Till Eulenspiegel

Frontispiece
(Eulenspiegel means "owl-mirror")

Till Eulenspiegel's Merry Pranks, Cheats and Devices

The Earliest Version of the Classic Legend

Written by N
Edited by Charles Siegel

Omo Press

adolescentium alunt
senectutem oblectant

ISBN 978-1-941667-24-8

Cover illustration: Till Eulenspiegel by Charles Henry Granger, mid-nineteenth-century American artist.

New material in this book,
including modernized spelling and punctuation, is
Copyright © 2019 by Omo Press. All rights reserved.

The History of this Book

In the 1400s, oral tales about Till Eulenspiegel spread through Germany.

In 1510, the first edition of the collected tales was printed by Johannes Gruninger in German under the title *Ein kurtzweilish lesen von Dyl Ohlenspiegel* (which means *An Amusing reading of Till Eulenspiegel*). It was reprinted several times during that decade, and the complete 1515 edition survives. In the preface, the anonymous author identified himself only as "N" and said that he began the very difficult project of collecting the oral tales in 1500.

The book was soon published in French, Dutch, and English, a sign of its popularity. The first English edition may have been as early as 1520, but it does not survive. It translated the name Eulenspiegel as "Howleglas" because the name literally means "Owl-mirror."

Between 1547 and 1568, William Copeland of London printed several editions that contained many tales from the German edition anonymously translated into English, again using the name Howleglas instead of Eulenspiegel. Copeland's editions differed from one another in minor ways, and some had illustrations while others did not.

In 1867, Frederic Ouvry, an English lawyer and antiquarian, reprinted Copeland's translation. At the time, only three copies from three of Copeland's editions survived, and none was complete. Ouvry combined them to create a complete text and published it with newly set type and without illustrations under the title "Howleglas."

This edition uses Ouvry's version of Copeland's text, and it includes woodcut illustrations from the German edition of 1515. It makes the following changes to Ouvry's text:
- Modernized spelling and punctuation: Copeland's archaic spelling is difficult, and his chaotic punctuation is even more difficult, to read. This edition modernizes spelling and punctuation to make the text accessible to today's readers.
- Modernized names: This edition uses the name "Eulenspiegel" instead of "Howleglas" because it is more familiar to modern readers. For the same reason, it uses modern place names, such as "Saxony" instead of Copeland's "Sassen," and it uses place names from the German text rather than Copeland's confusing Anglicization of them, such as "Nuremberg" rather than Copeland's "Northborough." Its title is based on the titles of later English editions rather than Ouvry's "Howleglas."
- Corrections to obvious errors: The text has a significant number of errors. It even leaves out a passage of one of the tales and instead duplicates the final hundred and one words of the tale in the location where that passage should be. There are also many small errors, such as using "they" instead of "the." This edition makes the minimal number of corrections needed to make the text coherent and consistent.

This modernized text should be easy for any English speaker to read. Archaic words are defined in footnotes the first time they appear. The following archaic words appear many times:
- "An" means "if."
- "Wist, wot" mean "know, knew."
- "Liever" means "rather."
- "Mete" means "measure."

The Tales

How Eulenspiegel as he was born was christened three times upon one day

In the land of Saxony, in the village of Knetlingen, there dwelt a man that was named Nicholas Eulenspiegel that had a wife named Wypeke that lay a childbed in the same village. And that child was borne to christening and named Till Eulenspiegel. And then the child was brought into a tavern where the father was with his gossips and made

good cheer. When the midwife had well drunk, she took the child to bear it home, and in the way was a little bridge over a muddy water. And as the midwife would have gone over the little bridge, she fell into the mud with the child, for she had a little drunk too much wine, for had not help come quickly they had both be drowned in the mud. And when they came home with the child, they made a kettle of warm water to be made ready and there they washed the child clean of the mud.

And thus was Eulenspiegel three times in one day christened: once at the church, once in the mud, and once in the warm water.

How that Eulenspiegel, when that he was a child, answered a man that asked the way

Upon a time went Eulenspiegel's father and mother out and left Eulenspiegel with the house. There came there a man riding half into the door and asked, "Is there nobody within?" Then answered the child that there is a half a man and a horse head.

Then asked the man, "Where is thy father?" And the child answered and said, "My father is of ill making worse, and my mother is gone for scath* or shame." And the man said to the child, "How understandest thou that?" And then the child said, "My father is making of ill worse, for he ploweth the field and maketh great holes that men should fall therein when they ride. And my mother is to borrow bread, and when she giveth it again and giveth less it is shame, and when she giveth it and giveth more that is scathe."

Then said the man, "Which is the way to ride?" And the child answered and said "There where the geese go." And then rode the man his way to the geese, and when he

---

* harm, injury

came to the geese they flew into the water. Then wist* he not where to ride but turned again to the child and said, "The geese be flown into the water, and thus wot I not what to do nor whither to ride." Then answered the child, "Thou must ride where the geese go, and not where they swim." Then departed the man and rode his way and marveled of the answer of the child.

How Eulenspiegel sat upon his father's horse behind him

Many great complaints came before the father of Eulenspiegel, how his son was a deceiver of folk and a great mocker. This complaint was made on him when he could go; and when he lay in the cradle, he tumbled upon the cushions with his arse upward; and when he came to the age of nine years old, he let no ungraciousness scape from him, in so much that all the neighbors complained on him.

Then said his father to him "How commeth this that the people complaineth so to me? They say that ye be a mocker and a deceiver." Then said Eulenspiegel, "Good father, I do nobody harm, and that shall I show unto you. Take a horse and go upon his back, and I will ride behind you. Then you shall see what the people will say to me." And then light his father upon his horse and took his son behind him. And when he was upon the horse, he showed the people his arse. Then said the folk, "What ungracious knave and beguiler is that." Then said Eulenspiegel to his father, "Now may thou hear, I hold my peace and speak never a word, and yet saith they that I am a knave and a deceiver of folk."

And then his father took him and set him before him on the horse, and then began he to grin and put out his tongue upon the people that his father saw not, and then the people said, "See what a cursed young knave is there." Then said

* knew

his father to Eulenspiegel, "Thou was born in an unhappy time, for now thou sittest before me and doest nobody harm, and yet for all that, they do call thee a knave and a beguiler."

And so departed Eulenspiegel's father out of the land of Megdburg, a village from thence where his wife was, and within short space died. And then abide Eulenspiegel's mother with him and ate and drank together such as they might get, for she was but poor. And Eulenspiegel would go to no craft, but when he was sixteen years old he began to dance upon a cord, and no otherwise.

How Eulenspiegel fell from the rope into the water whereof the people had good sport

Upon a time Eulenspiegel played upon the cord that was set over the water, where he made good sport, but at the last there was one that cut the rope, so fell he into the water and was all too wet, and he came out as well as he might. For the little spite, he thought to quite* them again, and said to them, "Come again tomorrow, and I will do many more wonders upon the rope."

And the next day after, came Eulenspiegel and danced upon the cord, and then he said to the young folk, "Ye shall see what news I can do. Give me every body your right shoe upon the rope end." So they did, and the old men also. And when he had danced a while he cast them their shoon† upon a heap and bade them take their shoon each of them again. Then ran they after their shoon and for haste one tumbled over the other. And then they began to lie together by the ears, and smite with their fists so hard that they fell to the earth. One said weeping, "This is my shoe," and the other laughed and cried, "That is my shoe." And thus for their shoon lay they together by the ears.

* requite, pay back
† shoes

Then began Eulenspiegel to laugh, crying, "Seek your shoon. Yesterday ye bathed me," and he leapt from the cord and went his way to his mother's and durst not come out again in the space of a month.

And so he tarried with his mother, whereof his mother was glad, but she knew not the cause why he did with her nor what he had done.

How Eulenspiegel's mother learned him and bade him go to a craft

Wybeke, the mother of Eulenspiegel, was glad that her son Eulenspiegel was so subtle and wise, and she said that he might not live so and get money as therewith. And then she said to her son that he should learn a craft. And then answered Eulenspiegel to his mother, "What thing is that that a body should dispose himself to that should abide by him all his life?"

And his mother answered clean contrary and said, "That me also thinketh, for in three days I had no bread in my house. Should I not abide and suffer all my life? I had liever* die."

Then said Eulenspiegel, "This is not an answer to my question, but I will answer now to yours," and said, "A poor man that hath nothing to eat, he must fast Saint Nicholas day, and he that hath meat may eat on Saint Martin's even. And in like wise it is with you."

How Eulenspiegel got bread for his mother

As Eulenspiegel's mother was thus without bread, then bethought Eulenspiegel how he might best get bread for her.

Then he went out of the village to a town thereby called Stassfurt, and went into a baker's house, where he asked the baker if he would send his lord for three shillings bread, some white and some rye. And he named a lord that was of another land, but he at that time was lodged at an inn in the town, and bade the baker let one go with him and that he should have his money, and the baker was content.

And then Eulenspiegel gave the baker a bag that had a hole in the bottom, and therein put he the bread and so departed with the bakers lad, and when he was in another street he let fall three white loaves at the hole in the dirt. And then bade Eulenspiegel to the baker's servant, "Set down the bag and go fetch me other white bread for this, for I dare not bear it to my lord." And then went the baker's servant home to change the bread, and in the meanwhile went Eulenspiegel with the sack of bread home to his mother's.

And when the baker's servant came again to the place and found not Eulenspiegel, he returned home again and told his master how Eulenspiegel had served him, and the

---

* rather

baker heard that Eulenspiegel was gone his way with his bread. Then ran the baker to the inn that Eulenspiegel named him and asked the servants of the lord for Eulenspiegel, but they said there came none such, and then knew the baker that he was deceived and so returned home.

Then said Eulenspiegel to his mother, eat and make merry now you have it, and when you have no more ye must fast.

How Eulenspiegel creeped into a bee hive, and how he was stolen in the night

Upon a time went Eulenspiegel with his mother to the dedication of the church. And there he drank so much that he was drunk, and then went he into a garden thereby where stood many bee hives, and there he sought where he might have a place to sleep in, and at the last he found an empty bee hive, wherein he put himself to sleep for that night.

Then came there in the dead of the night two thieves for to steal away the hives, and they felt which of the hives was heaviest, for they thought therein was most honey, so at the last they felt the hive that Eulenspiegel was in, and then said the thief to his fellow, "Here is one that is very heavy. This will I have. Take thou another and let us go." Then took they the beehives on their necks and departed.

Then awoke Eulenspiegel and heard all what they said, and it was so dark that the one knew not the other. Then put Eulenspiegel his head out of the hive, and pulled the foremost by the hair wherewith he was angry, and said to his fellow behind him, "Why pullest ye me by the hair?" And then he answered, "I pull thee by the hair, and I have as much as I can do to bear my hive." And within a while after, he pulled the hindermost by the hair, that was right angry and said, "I bear so heavy that I sweat, and for all that thou pullest me by the hair." Then answered the foremost, "Thou liest, how should I pluck thee by the hair, and I can scantly

find my way."

And thus went the chiding by the way; and as they were chiding, Eulenspiegel put out his hand again and pulled the foremost by the hair, whereof he was angry and set down his hive and took his fellow by the head, and thus they tumbled together by the hair in the street, and at the last when the one had well beaten the other, they ran their way and left the hives lying, and then slept Eulenspiegel in the bee hive till in the morning, and then he arose and went forth, and as he went he came by a castle and went in, and the lord asked him if he would have a master and he said yes, and then the lord hired him.

And upon a time he rode with his master by the way where stood hemp. Then said his master to him, "When thou findest such seed, shit therein, for therewith men be hanged upon the gallows and upon the wheels, both thieves and murderers." Then answered Eulenspiegel that he would do it, and his master said so because that he was a thief and in the night went a robbing and a stealing, for he lived almost thereby.

On a time as his master was at supper, the cook called Eulenspiegel and bade him go into the cellar and fetch him the mustard out of the pot. And then went Eulenspiegel and he understood that the cook bade him go fetch a hempen rope. Then marveled he what he meant for he never saw none afore. Then thought he, will he bind me therewith? Then went Eulenspiegel into the cellar, and there he sought about, and at the last he found the pot with mustard, and then he remembered him and said, "My master bade me that where I found any such seed that I should shit therein," and then he put his arse over the pot and shit therein a great heap, and then he stirred it about together and brought it to the cook, and then the cook dressed the mustard in saucers and send them to the table and the lord tasted, and it savored ill. Then said he to the cook, "What have you ground in the mustard, for it savoreth like as there were a turd therein?"

And then began Eulenspiegel to laugh. Then said his master, "Whereat laughest thou? Thinkest thou we cannot taste, then taste thou." And then answered Eulenspiegel, "I eat no mustard, for wote you not what you bade me do when that we rode over such seed, that when I found such seed you said that then I should shit in it, for with such seed you said men were hanged: and so have I shitten in the seed." Then said his master, "O thou unhappy knave, this seed is not like the seed of hemp; but I know this by very good reason that thou hast done it of cursedness and great falseness," and then he took a staff and would have smited Eulenspiegel.

And then Eulenspiegel took his legs and ran away, and his master after him, but he could not overtake him. Then he returned home again, and Eulenspiegel would no more come there.

How Eulenspiegel was hired of a priest

As Eulenspiegel ran out of the castle, he came to a village that was called Buddensteten in the land of Brunswick. And there came a priest to Eulenspiegel and hired him, but he knew him not, and the priest said to him that he should have good days and eat and drink the same meat that he himself and his woman did, and all that should be done with half the labor, and then said Eulenspiegel that thereafter would he do his diligence.

Then dressed the priest's woman two chickens, and she bade Eulenspiegel turn and so he did, and he looked up and saw that she had but one eye, that when the chickens were enough, then he broke one of the chickens from the spit, and ate it without any bread. And when it was dinner time, came the woman into the kitchen where Eulenspiegel turned and thought to take up the chickens; and when

she was come, she found no more there but one chicken. Then said she to Eulenspiegel, "Where is the other chicken? There were two chickens." Then answered he to her, "Lift up your eye, and then you shall see the other chicken." Then was the woman therewith angry and knew well that Eulenspiegel mocked her, and then she ran to the priest and told him how she had dressed two chickens, and while she came to take them up she found but one, and then he mocked me because I had but one eye. Then went the priest to Eulenspiegel and said, "Why mock ye my woman? There was two chickens." Then answered Eulenspiegel and said that was truth, "I have said to the woman that she should open her eyen, and she should see well where that other chicken was become."

Then laughed the priest and said, "She cannot see. She hath but one eye." Then said Eulenspiegel to the priest, "The one chicken have I eaten, for ye said that I should eat and drink as well as you and your woman, and the one I ate for you and the other I ate for your woman, for I was afraid that you should have sinned for the promise that ye promised me, and therefore I made measure."

Then said the priest, "I care not for the chickens but I would have you please my woman and do after her." Then said Eulenspiegel, "I do your commandment," and that the woman bade him do, he did but half; for she bade him fetch a bucket of water, and he went and brought it but half full of water; and when he should bring two logs, he brought but one; and when he should give the beasts two bundles of hay, he gave them but one; and when he should fetch a pot full of beer, he brought it half full; and so did he of many other things more.

Then complained she to the priest of Eulenspiegel again. Then said the priest, "I bade that you should do as she bade you," and Eulenspiegel answered, "I have done as ye bade me, for ye said to me that I should do all thing with half labor and your woman would fain see with both eyes, but she seeth but with one eye, and so do I half the labor." And then the priest laughed, and then said the woman, "Will you have this ungracious knave any longer, then will not I tarry no longer with you but depart."

Then gave the priest Eulenspiegel leave to depart for his woman's sake. But when the parish clerk was dead of the village, then sent the priest for Eulenspiegel and holp him so much that that he was made the parish clerk.

How Eulenspiegel was made clerk of Buddensteten

As Eulenspiegel was clerk of the church, he should help the priest to sing mass, and as he stood afore the altar with the priest, the priest let a great fart that all the church rang thereof. Then said Eulenspiegel, "Sir parson, what offer you there our lord for frankincense!" Then answered the parson,

"What hast thou to do therewith, for I have the power to shit in the midst of the church, and I will."

Then said Eulenspiegel "I hold a barrel of beer that you shall not shit in the middle thereof." Then said the priest, "I hold you. Think you that I am not so hardy nor bold to do that?" Then turned the parson him about and went and shit in the church a great heap and said, "Clerk, I have won the barrel of beer." Then said Eulenspiegel, "Yet ye have not, for we will first mete* whether it be in the midst of the church or not." And then they met it, and it lacked of the middle more than six feet, and then won Eulenspiegel the barrel of beer, whereof the priest's leman† was angry and said, "You will keep this ungracious knave so long with you that at the last he will shame you."

And then in the mean season while Eulenspiegel was parish clerk, at Easter they should play the resurrection of

---

* measure
† In this case, "leman" means "woman."

our lord; and for because that the men were not learned nor could not read, the priest took his leman and put her in the grave for an angel. And this seeing, Eulenspiegel took to him two of the simplest persons that were in the town, that played the three Maries, and the parson played Christ, with a banner in his hand; then said Eulenspiegel to the simple persons, "When the angel asketh you whom you seek, you may say, the parson's leman with one eye." Then it fortuned that the time was come that they must play and the angel asked them who they sought, and then said they as Eulenspiegel had showed and learned them afore, and then answered they, "We seek the priest's leman with one eye," and then the priest might hear that he was mocked.

And when the priest's leman heard that, she arose out of the grave and would have smitten with her fist Eulenspiegel upon the cheek, but she missed him and smote one of the simple persons that played one of the three Maries, and he gave her another, and then took she him by the hair, and that seeing his wife came, running hastily to smite the priest's leman, and then the priest seeing this cast down his banner, and went to help his woman, so that the one gave the other sore strokes and made great noise in the church.

And then Eulenspiegel, seeing them lying together by the ears in the body of the church, went his way out of the village and came no more there.

How that Eulenspiegel would fly from the town's house of Megdburg

After that came Eulenspiegel to Megdburg, where he did many marvelous things, yet his name was there well known. Then bade the principal of the town, that he should do some thing that was never seen before. Then said he that he would go to the highest of the council house, and fly from it, and anon* that was known through all the town that

* soon

Eulenspiegel would fly from the top of the council house, in such that all the town was there assembled and gathered in the market place to see him. Upon the top of the house stood Eulenspiegel with his hands wavering as though he would have flyen, and then the people looked when he should have flied, whereat he laughed and said to the people, "I thought there had been no more fools but myself, but I see well that here is a whole town full. For had ye altogether said that ye would have flied, that I would not have believed you. And now ye believe one fore that saith that he will fly, which thing is unpossible for I have no wings, and no man can fly without wings."

And then went he his way from the top of the council house and left the folk there standing. And then departed the folk from thence, some blaming him and some laughing, saying he is a shrewd fool for he telleth us the truth.

How Eulenspiegel made himself a physician, and how he beguiled a doctor of the Bishops of Megdburg

The bishop Bruno of Megdburg, Earl of Querfurt, and all his nobles loved Eulenspiegel for that he did many proper conceits, and therefore the Bishop gave him meat and drink, clothes and wages.

The bishop had a right wise doctor with him, and he in no wise might hear nor see fools. So upon a time as he saw Eulenspiegel there he said to the bishop and the lord's men, "You should let come in Lords' Courts wise men and no fools; for the wise men will be conversant with wise men and give wise reasons, and fools will be conversant with fools and give foolish reasons."

And then answered they and said that reason is false, for he that foolishness will not hear nor see, he may well depart from them. There be also that think themself wise that be often times defiled of fools. It belongs to princes, lords, and barons, to have in their courts fools, for often times they drive away heavy thoughts and fantasies and melancholy. Where lords be, there will be also fools.

Then said Eulenspiegel to the lords, "What argument have you had with the doctor for my sake forsooth he shall be quit and you will help me thereto"; and they said all yes.

Then departed he out of the court by the space of three weeks, and then came again to Megdburg, and then he came to the lodging there where the doctor layeth and was sick, for the which sickness he sought for help. Then said the lords that there was come a cunning man and a master of physic that had helped many people. The doctor knew not Eulenspiegel, and then he took him by the arm and led him into his lodging, where he spake to him and said, "An* ye can help me, I shall content you well for your labor." Then answered he, "I trust to help you, but first I must lie by you

* if

one night, that I may cover you well that you may sweat, and by the air of the sweat I shall well know what sickness it is that you have." And that the priest, weening* that all had been true, granted to him. And then gave Eulenspiegel to him a strong purgation for to make him shit, but he said to the doctor that it was a medicine to make him to sweat, and the doctor believed him. And then went Eulenspiegel into the garden, and there stood a pot, the which Eulenspiegel took and shit in, and he took the pot and put it between the bed and the wall of the doctor, that the doctor knew it not, and the doctor went afore to bed. And then came Eulenspiegel to bed, and the priest turned him to the wall where the pot stood, and then he felt such a stink of the dirt that stood in the pot, so that he turned his head again toward Eulenspiegel. Then let Eulenspiegel a great stinking fart, and then turned the doctor again toward the wall, and

* believing

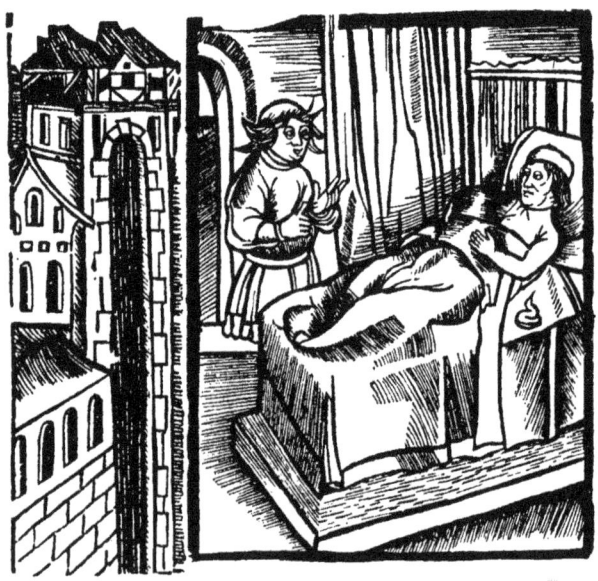

then stank the dirt in the pot. And thus suffered the doctor the stink half the night that he thought his heart did break, and then began the medicine to work so much that he beshit all the bed. Then said Eulenspiegel, "How do the master doctor. Methink your sweat stinketh very sore." The doctor thought in his mind, that know I well enough, but he might not speak because of the stink.

Then said Eulenspiegel, "I will go fetch you a candle and see how it is with you," and as he rose he let a great fart. Then said the doctor, "Alas I die." But he thanked God that Eulenspiegel was gone, that he might have some air. Then began the day to appear, and so departed Eulenspiegel his way. And then looked the doctor by the bed's side and there found the pot of dirt that stank so, and then took he it and cast it away, and then knew he well that he was mocked.

And within a while came the bishop and his nobles to visit the doctor, and when they came to his chamber, they asked him how he fared, and he answered and said, "Never worse, for I am almost dead." Then they told the bishop how the master of physic had served him, and then began the bishop to laugh and all his lords, and said, "This cometh to pass all after your words, for ye said that fools would have conversation with fools and give foolish reasons, and wise men would have conversation with wise men and give wise reasons. But I see that many wise be made fools of fools, and so be you, for if that ye would have suffered Eulenspiegel and said nothing, ye had not been mocked of him. For the physician that was with you was Eulenspiegel, and that we all knew well enough but in no wise† we would show you, for because ye were so wise that ye should be beguiled of a fool. For there is no man that is wise but he must know fools, for where no fools be, how should men know wise folk?" And then the doctor held his peace and

* by
† way

spake no more, and then never after durst he complain more of fools, but let them do all that they would after their own mind.

How Eulenspiegel made a sick child shit that afore might not shit, and how he got great worship thereof and praise

Men let alone and take no heed of cunning men yet dwell by them but proffer them a little or naught for their labor, nor be beloved, but rural persons and vagabonds have all their desire — as it is done to Eulenspiegel, that came into the land of Hildesheim, in a lodging where the good man was not at home, but Eulenspiegel was welcome to the goodwife of the house.

In the house there was a sick child lying by the fire, and then Eulenspiegel seeing the child lie so, he asked his hostess what sickness that the child had. Then answered the woman to Eulenspiegel and said, "If the child might go to the draught, he should do well enough. And then answered Eulenspiegel thereto, "Know you no remedy?" Then answered the woman, "Can ye help the child? An ye can, I shall give you that ye shall be pleased therewith." Then answered Eulenspiegel, "That is but a little thing to do, nor no cunning, for I will take nothing therefore."

And so departed the wife into the garden, and in the meanwhile, did Eulenspiegel shit a green turd, and then set the shitting chair over the turd and set the child thereon, as though the child had done it. Then came the woman out of the garden and asked who had done that, and then answered Eulenspiegel, "I have done it. Ye said that the child could not go to the draught, therefore I have set the child in the chair." Then took the woman the child away and saw so much dirt underneath. Then said she to Eulenspiegel, "This is it that hath hindered the child so long. For this great cure ye must have great thank thereof." Then

said Eulenspiegel, "Such mastery can I do with less cost." Then said the woman, "I pray you learn me that cunning, and I will give you therefore what you will have." Then said Eulenspiegel, "I must needs depart from hence, but when I come again I will learn you that science and learning," and then went he into the stable and saddled his horse and took his leave and so departed from thence. But he taught not his hostess that science but so departed.

How Eulenspiegel made whole all the sick folk that were in the hospital, where the spear of our lord* is

Upon a time Eulenspiegel came to Nuremberg, and he set upon the church doors and upon the Guild hall, and every place that all the people in that town might know, that he

* A relic in Nuremberg was believed to be the spear that pierced Jesus' side on the cross.

was a great master of physic, that all sick he could make whole. And then the master of the hospital house, where the spear of our Lord is, had many sick folks in his house. Then went the master of the hospital to Eulenspiegel and asked him if he could help sick men or lame men and make them whole, and he would reward him after his own pleasure. Then answered Eulenspiegel to the master of the hospital, "Will ye give me two hundred gold guldens, and I shall recover and make them whole of all the sickness and diseases, and will have no month till all the sick persons be delivered out of the hospital." These words pleased the master of the hospital very well, and he gave him some money in his hand.

Upon the morrow after came Eulenspiegel to the hospital with two men after him, and then he asked the sick folk, one after the other, what disease they had, and when he had asked them all, then he made them swear

upon a book that they should keep his counsel whatsoever he said to them. They answered that they would. Then said Eulenspiegel to them, "I have undertaken to make you all whole which is unpossible, but I must needs burn one of you all to powder, and then must I take the powder of him and give all the others to drink thereof, with other medicines that I shall minister thereto. And he that is the last, when I shall call you out of the hospital, and he that cannot go, shall be he that shall be burned. For on Wednesday next coming, then shall I come before the master of the hospital, and then shall I call and he that sleepeth longest shall pay for all."

Then prepared every one of the sick folk their crutches, that they would not be the last. And when Eulenspiegel was come to the masters of the hospital, then called he them, and then they ran out of the hospital, and some of them had not been out of their bed ten year before. Then when the sick folk were out of the hospital, then asked he his money, and then the master gave it him and then he departed.

And within three days after came again the poor men to their hospital and complained of their sickness, and then the master of the hospital said to them, "How cometh this to pass? I gave the master of physic a great sum of money to make you whole." Then answered the poor folk, "He hath deceived you and us both. For four day past, he come to every one of us and said to us that he should come on Wednesday next coming and heal us, but he said he must needs first burn one of us, and said that should be he that, when he should call, should be the last out of his bed, and the powder of him should they drink and be made whole therewith.

Then knew the master of the hospital that he was deceived and beguiled, and then took he the poor folk from the hospital and put every one in their bed as they were before, but he did all against his will.

How that a baker hired Eulenspiegel to be his servant

Upon a time came Eulenspiegel to a baker for to dwell, and the baker had need of a servant, and then he hired Eulenspiegel.

In the next morning after, must the baker bake, so the night before must Eulenspiegel sift the meal without a candle. Then said he to his master, "Ye must given me a candle." Then answered the baker, "I never gave a candle to boult* with, but they did boult in the moonlight. Then answered Eulenspiegel, "I am content." Then went his master to bed to sleep three hours, and in the meanwhile, let he the boulting bag out of the window in the moonshine, and then began he to boult the flour upon the earth in the garden. Then arose his master and thought to have baken and came to the boulting house, and then he saw that Eulenspiegel had boulted the meal in the garden upon the bare ground.

* sift

Then said the baker to Eulenspiegel, "What the devil doest thou think, the meal cost no more but strawing upon the earth?" Then answered Eulenspiegel to his master, "I have done as ye told me, for it is boulted in the moonshine." Then answered the baker, "I bade thee that thou shouldest boult it by the moonshine." And then answered Eulenspiegel, "So have I done, for it is sifted in the moonshine, and without the moonshine."

And then said Eulenspiegel, "There is not much meal lost, but that we may take it up again." And then answered the baker, "It is too late now for to bake, for our dough is not made." Then answered Eulenspiegel to his master and said, "I shall help you well. Your neighbor hath dough ready made in the kneading trough, and I will go fetch that and put yours in the stead." Then was the baker much angry and bade him go to the gallows and fetch what was under it,* and then said Eulenspiegel he would, and then he departed to the gallows, and when he came there he found nothing else but a few bones, and those he took up and brought home with him, and then said to his master, "I have brought that that I have found under the gallows. What will ye do with it?" Then was the baker more angry and said, "I shall complain on thee. Ye hast stolen away the kings justice." — then went out to the market and Eulenspiegel followed.

And then came the baker to the burgess of the town, and began to complain. And then came Eulenspiegel and stood by the baker, and therewith was the baker so angry that he wist† not what to say to the burgess and said angrily to Eulenspiegel, "What wilt thou have?" Then said Eulenspiegel, "I must needs see the complaint that ye make on me." Then answered the baker, "Go out of my sight, thou ungracious knave." Then answered Eulenspiegel to the

---

* The baker is dismissing Eulenspiegel, but Eulenspiegel takes his statement literally.
† knew

baker, "If I were in thy eyes, then must I needs pass through thy nostrils, when thou shuttest thy eyes."

Then departed the burgess, and knew well what he mocked. And then showed Eulenspiegel his arse to the baker, and asked him if he could bake such a loaf in his mouth. And then departed he and left the baker standing in the market place.

How Eulenspiegel was put in wages with the earl of Anhalt for to watch upon a tower to see when his enemies came and for to blow an horn to warn them thereof

Upon a time the earl of Anhalt hired Eulenspiegel, for he had many enemies and for that cause he must have many soldiers in wages that he must give meat to. But Eulenspiegel, that was in the top of the tower, was not of the merest,* for he was forgot.

Upon a time came his enemies, and fetched away a great stock of the earl's beasts, and that saw Eulenspiegel, but he held his peace, and that was spied and showed to the earl. And then the earl asked him, why he did lie so still and blew not. Then answered Eulenspiegel, "I did dance for my meat." Then said the earl, "Will ye not blow enemies?" Then answered Eulenspiegel, "I dare not, the field is so full of enemies, for if I should blow, they would come and slay you at your own gate." And then the earl was content and departed.

And within a while after was Eulenspiegel again forgot. And when the earl was at dinner and had great dainties before him, Eulenspiegel blew enemies. And by and by the earl and all his soldiers rose from the table, and dressed them in harness and ran to the gate, but they found no enemies. In the meanwhile took Eulenspiegel as much meat

---

* did not get even the smallest amount of meat.

as he would have from the earl's table. Then the soldiers and the earl came in and called Eulenspiegel to them, and the earl asked him why he blew enemies and there were none. The earl said it was a traitorous deed, and then he put him out of office. Then must he needs run with his footmen to fight with their enemies. Then said he that, for thinketh me, I would I were hence, but he could not.

Upon a time came enemies. Then went the soldiers out upon them, and Eulenspiegel was last; and when they returned again, he was the first in at the gate. At the last the earl had knowledge and came to Eulenspiegel and asked what was the cause that he was the last out and the first in. Then answered Eulenspiegel to the earl, "Worshipful lord, if it please you, when your soldiers made good cheer, I stood upon the tower fasting, and therefore I am not so strong as your soldiers be, and that is cause that I am last out and the first in. An you will give me meat enough as ye do the other, then shall I be the first." Then answered the earl, "Thinkest thou that I will keep thee so long as I have kept thee to do nothing but mock us in this manner, as ye have done so often?" Then gave he Eulenspiegel leave to depart, whereof he was very glad, for he loved no fighting and so departed he.

How Eulenspiegel won the king's fool of Casimir of Poland* with a great point of foolishness

King Casimir had with him a certain fool, which fool could play upon the fiddle, wherefore the king loved him much and set great price by him. Also the king heard oftentimes tell of Eulenspiegel, but he never could see him. And on a time it fortuned that Eulenspiegel came into the king's place for to ask dwelling, whereof when that the king wist that Eulenspiegel was come there to dwell, he was very glad thereof, and took him in and made him goodly cheer.

So it fortuned that the kings fool and Eulenspiegel could not agree, and that spied the king well and thought in his mind, what shall I do? And then he made the both to be brought before him in the hall and then he said to them, "Which of you two can the most foolishness? An one of you do that the other will not do, I shall give him new clothing and twenty ducats, and let it be done in my presence, before me and all my lords in this hall."

And then they answered both to the king that they would prepare them, and within a while, they came before the king and his lords. And then they began to do many proper conceits and merry touches of foolishness, one to the other, whereat the king and his lords had good laughter

---

* Casimir the Great was king of Poland from 1333 to 1370, the time when Eulenspiegel supposedly lived.

and good pastime thereat, for to see how the one labored for to overcome the other and to win the new clothes and the twenty ducats.

Then thought Eulenspiegel, this is good for me. Then he thought in his mind how he might do a thing that the other fool would not do. And then came he before the king and his lords, and before them all he did shit a great turd. And when he had done so, he took a spoon and divided it in the midst with the spoon, and when he had done so, he came to king's fool and said, "Do thou as I have done. Shit here in the midst, and when that the have done divide it in the midst, and take the spoon and take the one half of my turd and eat it, and I shall take the one half of thy turd and eat it." Then answered the king's fool that had I liever then I would eat half thy turd, or that mine own, I had liever all the days of my life go naked.

Then gave the king and all the lords the mastery to Eulenspiegel, and they gave him the new clothes and the twenty ducats. Then took he his leave and thanked the king, and so departed he from thence.

How the Duke of Lunenburg
banished Eulenspiegel out of his land

It befell on a time in the land of Lunenburg that Eulenspiegel had done a great fault and an unhappy touch to the duke, whereof the duke bade him that he should go out of his land and never after to come more therein; for if he were found there ever after to come more, he should lose his head. And then departed Eulenspiegel out of the Duke's land, for he durst no longer tarry there, for the strait commandment that the duke had commanded him.

And within a while after it fortuned that Eulenspiegel's way lay so, that he must pass through the duke's land of which he was banished, to go to the place where him lust[*] best. And as he passed through the duke's land it fortuned that he spied the duke riding toward him, so that he could no way pass but he must needs see him. Then lighted Eulenspiegel down from his horse that he rode on and drew out his knife and cut the horse's throat. And then he turned his horse's belly, and ripped out all the bowels of his horse, and cast them away, and then he set the horse with his belly upward, and went and stood therein.

And within a while after came the duke riding by, and as he passed by one of the duke's servants spied him standing in the horse's belly, and he rode to the duke and showed to him where that Eulenspiegel stood. Then rode the duke to him, and when he came to him he said, "Who made thee so bold as to enter into my land?"

---

* pleased

Then Eulenspiegel said, "Worshipful lord, I desire you thee pardon of my life, for when I saw you not far from me, then put I myself in my horse belly. For I have heard say that every man in his own ground is free, and now I stand in my own ground and not in yours."

Then laughed the duke and said, "I give the pardon go out of the dead horse and do as ye were wont to do," and so departed the duke. And then said Eulenspiegel to his horse, "I thank thee for thou hast saved my life and caused the duke to give me pardon." And so departed Eulenspiegel.

How Eulenspiegel took upon him to be a painter

Then it fortuned that Eulenspiegel might no longer tarry in the land of Saxony for his knavishness.

Then departed he into the land of Hesse to Megdburg to the earl, and he asked Eulenspiegel what occupation he was of? Then answered Eulenspiegel, "Worshipful lord, I am a painter. My cunning doth excel all others, for in no land is not for cunning as I." Then answered the earl, "Have you here any example of your work?" Then answered Eulenspiegel to the earl, "Yes my lord." Then had he been in Flanders, and brought with him diverse images that pleased the earl wonderful well.

Then said the earl to Eulenspiegel, "Master, what shall I give to you to take upon you to paint upon the wall in my hall, all the lords, and knights of my progeny, from the first unto the last, in the goodliest and fairest manner that ye can, with all the earls of Hesse and their ladies with them, and how our forefathers were married to ladies of strange lands. And all this must you cast that it may be upon the walls of my hall."

Then answered Eulenspiegel to the earl, "Worshipful lord, if it please you that you will have all this that you have rehearsed to me to be painted so costly and richly as you speak of, then would it cost, only the colors that should long thereto above, three hundred gold guldens."

Then answered the earl to Eulenspiegel and said, "Make it well, and in the best manner that you can, and we twain shall agree after the best manner. And also I shall do you a greater pleasure then all that come thee to."

And then took Eulenspiegel the work upon him, but he said to the lord that he must needs have an hundred guldens in earnest to buy the colors that belonged thereto and for his men's' wages. And then bade the earl the rent master give to Eulenspiegel an hundred guldens, and so he did. Then went Eulenspiegel and got him three fellows, and then came he again to the earl and asked him a boon before he began to work, and the earl granted him; and then he did ask of the earl that there should no person be so hardy to come into the hall to trouble him and his workmen without they ask him license. And the earl granted his desire.

And then went Eulenspiegel into the hall with his servants, and when he and they were in the hall, Eulenspiegel set a pair of tables before them and he bade them play, but he made them before to swear that they should not bewray him. And the fellows had good pastime, wherewith they were well content and glad that they might have meat, drink, and clothes, and do no other thing but play and pass the time in that manner. And Eulenspiegel did no other thing but hang a white cloth before the wall. That done, he came and played with his servants.

In mean time, longed the earl greatly to see his work, if it were so goodly as the copy was, and to see if the colors were good, and so he departed and came to Eulenspiegel and said, "Good master painter, I pray you let me go with you to see your work." Then said Eulenspiegel to the lord, "Worshipful lord, before that you see my work, I must show to you one thing. He the which is not born in wedlock may not see my painting." Then said the earl, "That were a marvelous thing."

And then went he with Eulenspiegel into the hall and there had he hanged up a white cloth that he should have painted. And he had in his hand a white rod, and he did away the cloth that hanged upon the wall and pointed upon the wall with his white rod, and showed the earl that that was the first lord of the land and earl of Hesse; and this is the earl of Rome, he had a wife that they called Justine, the Duke's daughter of Benem, and after he was made emperor; and of the daughter of him came Adolphus; and of Adolphus came William the swart; and this William had one Lewis; so forth to your noble grace. And I know well that there is no person living that can deprove my works, so curiously have I made, and with fair colors."

But the Lord saw no work but the plain wall. Then thought he in his mind, am I a bastard, is my mother a whore? I see nothing but the white wall.

And for because that he would not be known for a bastard, he said to Eulenspiegel, "Master, your work pleaseth me marvelously well, but my understanding is very small therein." And with that, he went out of the hall and came to his wife, and she asked him how that work did please him. He said, "I have shrewd trust in him." Then said the earl, "I like it well. Shall it please you to look thereon?" And she granted, and then she desired Eulenspiegel that she might see his work, and he granted her and then said unto her secretly as he had said before to her lord, and showed her the lords upon the wall with the white rod in his hand as he did to the lord. And there stood one foolish gentlewoman with the lady, and she said, that she saw no painting on the wall, and the other spake not one word. And then thought Eulenspiegel, will this fool tell truth? — then must I needs depart. Then hanged he up the white cloth and so departed the lady.

And when she was come to her lord, he asked her how she liketh the work, she said, "How that it liketh me, it liketh not my foolish gentlewoman." And she said that some of her gentlewomen said that it was but deceit, and so thought the lord.

Then said the lord to Eulenspiegel that he should make ready his work that he and his lords might see it tomorrow that he might know which of them were born in wedlock and which were not, for he that is not born in wedlock, all his land is forfeit to me.

Then answered Eulenspiegel, "I will do it with a good will." Then went he to the rent master, and received of him a hundred gold guldens. And when he had received the money, he said to his servants, "Now must we all depart," and gave them money, of the which they were content and so departed.

Then on the morrow came the earl with his lords into the hall and the asked where the master painter was and his company, for he said he would see the work. Then turned he up the cloth and asked them an they saw any work and they said nay. Then said the earl, "We be deceived." He said, "We have sore longed to see Eulenspiegel, and now he hath beguiled us, but it maketh no great matter for the money. But let us banish him from our land for a beguiler of people," and so they did. And so departed the earl with his lords.

How Eulenspiegel had many and great disputations with all the noble doctors of Prague in Bohemia

Then departed Eulenspiegel from the land of Hesse, and then came he to Prague in Bohemia, where was an university of scholars and students, of doctors and bachelors.

Then made Eulenspiegel bills and set them upon every church door, and he wrote that he would answer to all manner of questions that were laid upon him and give answer thereto. And as he had set up the bills, then came the scholars of the university and read them. And when they had read them and found therein that he should give an answer to all that was asked him, then took they a bill and went to the rector and showed him that there was one come that had set us these letters upon the church doors, and he saith therein that he will give answer to all manner of questions that were put to him. Then the rector hearing this sent a scholar to the place where Eulenspiegel was lodged, and charged the host of the house that he should tomorrow bring with him the man that had set up the bills upon pain that should fall thereafter. And then the host answered he would. Then departed the scholar home.

Then on the morrow came Eulenspiegel and his host to the university with two or three of his neighbors. And when they were come, then was Eulenspiegel taken by the arm and set in a chair. And then came the rector with many doctors, and shortly they were set about him. Then asked they him how many gallons of water was in the sea? Then answered Eulenspiegel, "Do stop all the rivers that run therein, and then I shall mete it, and then shall I show you how many there be." Then thought the rector that was unpossible to do, but he was content with the answer.

Then asked he Eulenspiegel the second answer, "How many days be past since Adam to this time?" And then answered Eulenspiegel to the rector, "It is eight days past and more, for when the week is done, then beginneth again the next week seven other days, and so forth the end of the world."

Then said the rector, "Tell me now the third answer," and Eulenspiegel bade him say what he would. Then asked the rector him, where was the middle of all the world, and then answered Eulenspiegel to the rector that is here in the midst of this house, for an you believe not me, then take a

cord and mete it, and if it lack a straw breadth, then will I be counted for an unlearned man.

And then the rector had liever give him the mastery then he would mete it, but then he waxed angry and asked him how far is the earth from heaven? Then answered Eulenspiegel, "That is hereby, for let men sing never so softly here but it is heard in heaven. An ye will not me believe, then take a ladder and go up into heaven, and I shall here speak softly, and if ye here it not, then will I lose the prize."

Then the rector said to Eulenspiegel, "How wide is all heaven, and how broad is it?" Then answered Eulenspiegel to the rector and said, "It is twelve thousand miles broad and ten thousand miles wide, and if ye will not me believe, then must ye take the sun and the moon and all the stars of heaven and then go mete them, and if you find it not as I say, then will I give the mastery to you, and I will be overcome."

Then the rector and the doctors knew not what they

should say more to Eulenspiegel, but they said that he was so subtle for them, and then they gave him the victory and praise. And then departed he out of the place, for he was afraid that they would have done to him some unhappiness.

How Eulenspiegel became a pardoner

As Eulenspiegel was known through all the country for his unhappy touches and beguiling that he had done to them, for that he was welcome to no place that he came to where he had been much made of before all in his youth. Then bethought Eulenspiegel in what manner he might get money with little labor.

Then went Eulenspiegel and got him a priest's gown, and dressed him like a scholar. Then went he into a certain churchyard where he found a dead man's head, and then he took the head up, and made it clean. And when it was clean he bare it to a certain goldsmith and bade him that he should band the head with silver bands, and he said that he would content him and so he did.

And when it was done, he contented the goldsmith, and then departed he to a village near thereby where it was the dedication day. And then came he to the parson of the church and saluted him, and then he told him that he had a relic, and he prayed the curate that he would do so much for him, that he would show it unto the parish, that they might offer to it. And he said to the parson that he should have the one half of the offering. And then the parson, moved with covetise, granted to him, for he was glad to get money.

Then told he to the people of his parish, "This man that here standeth hath brought a precious relic. He that offereth thereto hath great pardon. He shall come into the pulpit and declare it unto you."

Then went Eulenspiegel into the pulpit and then told he the people of the relic that he had there, and he said that the head spake to him and that it bade him that he should build a church over him and that the money that the church should be builded with should be well gotten.

And when the men and the women should come offer, then said Eulenspiegel to the women, all those that have made their husbands cuckolds should sit still and come not to offer, for the head bade him that it should not receive the offering. And then he came down out of the pulpit, and when he was come down, then came the poor men and their wives and offered to the head. And there was not one woman but she offered because that he had said so, and he gave them the blessing with the head. And there were some that had no money and they offered their rings, and some of them offered twice or thrice because they would be seen, and when they were gone there pressed fresh.

And thus received he their offering both of the good and of the ill, so that he had got a great some of money by that said practice. And when they had all offered, and that there

was no more that came, then he said to them, "All the men and women that here hath come and offered to this head be honest and good, and moreover I charge you on pain of cursing that there be not one of you that the other slander or backbite, for if you had not been good and honest, I should not have received your offering." And when the poor men of the country heard Eulenspiegel speak in this manner, they believed him.

And when the mass was done, then came the parson to Eulenspiegel and said to him that he should give to him half of the offering, and then divided Eulenspiegel the offering and gave the parson a part thereof that the parson was well content therewith, and then departed Eulenspiegel from the parson. And then the women thereabout were very glad of Eulenspiegel and made much of him, so abode he long with them and spent none of his money. In such manner could he cloak and hide his unhappiness and falseness.

How Eulenspiegel came to the town of Bamberg and how he did eat for money

Upon a time came Eulenspiegel from Nuremberg to Bamberg, where he entered into a lodging where was a merry hostess that bade Eulenspiegel often times welcome, for she saw by his clothing that he was a merry guest.

And as dinner time came the hostess asked him if that he would go to dinner, and she asked him also if it pleased him to be at the twelve penny table. Then answered Eulenspiegel and said to his hostess, "I am but a poor man. I pray you for God's sake to give me my dinner." Then said the hostess, "The baker and the butcher will not be so paid, and therefore must I have money, for there is none in my house but they eat and drink all for money." Then answered Eulenspiegel, "For money do men eat and drink. In good faith, so will

I." Then answered the woman to him, "What table will you be at? For at the lords' table they give me no less then two shillings, and at the merchants' table sixteen pence, and at my household servants give me twelve pence." Then answered Eulenspiegel to his hostess, "Sith* I must needs eat and pay money, then give me the best meat that you have." And then he set him down at the lords' table.

And then his hostess brought to the table, the best meat, and drink that she had, and she bade him make good cheer. She said "Oft much good do it you, gentle sir," and Eulenspiegel thanked his hostess many times. He ate and drank, and made him well at ease, and he ate so much of the good meat that he sweat again. When he had made him well at ease and ate and drunken all that he would, then bade he his hostess too avoid† the table, for he said, he must depart from thence, And right shortly at his commandment,

* since
† clear, empty

the table was avoided, and so he arose and stood by the fire, and when he was thorough warm he took his leave with his hostess and would have departed.

That seeing, the hostess took him by the sleeve and bade him to give her two shillings for his dinner. Then answered he, "God thank you, for you have remembered me, I must have two shillings of you. For you said to me that there came no manner of persons within your house but that they ate for money. And when you had told me that, I sat me down and said I would do the same. And I ate so much that I sweat again, and therefore you give money." Then said his hostess, "Must I give the money to eat my meat and drink my drink such guests,* I may have great piety. Pay me my money shortly, for the bakers and brewers will not be so answered." Then answered Eulenspiegel to his hostess, "Give me money, for thinkest thou that I will eat so much and labor myself so sore as I did, not to be paid for my labor? That I had much liever never to have seen thee nor thy house, for I have eaten so much for money that my belly is like to burst. Would you that I should have such great labor and not to pay therefore? I have other things to do than to stand that right here with thee, and therefore come off lightly and give me my money, and let me be gone, for I have right well deserved it." Then said his hostess to him, "Sir you have eaten my meat and drunk my drink, and by my fire you have had your ease and all at your own desire, wherefore I pray you to give me money." And he answered right angrily, "Would ye have me to pay money, and I did eat therefore, the which is to my great harm?" Then she answered to Eulenspiegel, "If your eating do you harm, I am not the cause thereof, but your eating is to my loss, not only that I have lost more then that cometh to."

And then she said, "Depart thou from my house and never after this that thou be so bold once to enter within my doors."

* If I must give such guests the money to eat...

Then said Eulenspiegel, "Will you on your conscience take my labor for nothing? Well, farewell." And then departed Eulenspiegel, and he was glad that he had so scaped from her, and she was glad that she was so delivered of him.

How Eulenspiegel went to Rome to speak with the Pope

Then when Eulenspiegel had long occupied his falseness, then he remembered this old proverb: I will to Rome my manners to amend, and home again my life for to end.

And then departed he to Rome, where he showed part of his ungraciousness. And when he came to Rome, he lodged with a widow, and the widow did oft behold him in the face, and because he was a fair young man, she said oft times, "Sir, you be right welcome. Good sir," she said "from whence be you?" "I am of Saxony, and my coming hither is for to speak with the Pope." Then answered she to Eulenspiegel, "Good friend, you may see him but you shall not speak with him. For I, that am born in Rome, would have given an hundred ducats to speak to him, but I could never speak to him." Then said Eulenspiegel, "Hostess, will you give an hundred ducats, and I shall bring you to the speech of the pope," and she sweared to him by her faith she would, for otherwise it would cost her more in gifts.

Then on a time should the pope sing mass his own person at Saint John Lateran, for every four weeks he must sing mass there. And as the pope was at mass, then Eulenspiegel drew near to the altar, and when the Pope was at the holy sacrament, then turned Eulenspiegel his back to the altar.

And that seeing, all the cardinals when mass was done they came to the pope, and they told to his grace that there stood a fair young man all the while that we were at mass and heard it devoutly till the time of the levation, and when that you lifted up the chalice above your head, then turned he his back toward the sacrament of the altar."

Then said the pope, "That is a thing to be looked on, for it is a great doubt whether that man believe well or not, and therefore it is needful for us to send for that man and to examine him what error it was that he held." The cardinals answered, that was the best. Then the pope sent for Eulenspiegel to his inn, and the messenger brought him to the pope, and when he came before the pope and the cardinals, they began straightly to examine him, and they asked of him what was his belief. Then answered Eulenspiegel to the pope, "I believe as a true Christian man ought for to believe, and I believe in Jesu Christ, and I believe that that our holy mother the church doth teach me, and I believe as my good hostess doth believe"; and he named her before the pope and all that whole congregation.

And then sent the pope a messenger to the inn where that Eulenspiegel was lodged, and when he was there he came to the hostess and bade her that she should make her

ready, for she must needs go with him to the pope, whereof she had great marvel and made her ready and so went with him to the pope. And when she was come before the pope, he asked her what her belief was. And she answered to the pope, "Reverend father, I believe as a true Christian woman should do, for I believe as the holy church believes, and also I believe in all that the holy church binds me to."

Then said Eulenspiegel, "The same believe I." Then the pope asked him why he turned his back to the holy sacrament when he did minister it. Then said Eulenspiegel to the pope, "Reverend father in God, I thought in my mind, when that thou lifted up the blessed sacrament, that I was not worthy it to behold nor thereon to look till the time that I was confessed and made clean of all my sins." And then was the Pope with that answer marvelously well contented and pleased.

And after that the pope bade him that he should confess him of his sins, and to make him clean thereof, and that said he gave his benediction to Eulenspiegel and his hostess, and so they twain departed. And shortly after departed the pope with all his cardinals into the palace, and so Eulenspiegel was quit thereof.

And then said Eulenspiegel to his hostess, "I must have my hundred ducats that I have earned." And then the woman gave him the hundred ducats, whereof he was glad, and he said to his self that he was the better for that journey to Rome.

How Eulenspiegel deceived the Jews with dirt

When Eulenspiegel the great deceiver had been at Rome, then came he to the town of Frankfurt, where a mart or a great market was kept. And as Eulenspiegel went about the market he spied a young man go with musk of Alexander to sell, that which was well sold and much set by.

Then said Eulenspiegel to his self, I will go with some merchandise for to sell, as well as that young man doth, and he thought in his mind how he might find some practice to get money without labor. Then thought he in his mind every night what was best to do, for the fleen* did bite him that he could not sleep. And he would right gladly have taken them, but he could not.

And when that the day began to spring, he arose and walked forth, and as he walked, then spied he by the way a fair fig tree, the which bore goodly fruit. And then he went and gathered two or three of them, and then he said to himself, this is good for my merchandise, and brought them with him into Frankfurt to the place where he was lodged, and he dressed them after his mind. And when he had dressed them, he put them in his arse and tempered them with his dirt and let them lie there by him by the space of two or three days, that they should not smell too much of dirt.

And in a morning betimes arose out of his bed and went to his hostess and hired a little table, and then he went into the market and bought two or three silken clothes, and there in a house he dressed these portingale figs that had lain so long in his arse with the silken clothes like as it had been the musk. Then took he his table and went into the market and set up his table. And when it was up, then showed he the portingale figs that he had made like as it had been musk.

Then came they many merchants of diverse lands to him, and they asked him what merchandise he had to sell, and he stood still and gave none of them no answer, whereof they marveled and so departed. And at the last there came to him two Jews, and they asked him what merchandise he had there to sell, and then answered Eulenspiegel to them and said, "This is a precious thing, for all those that do eat of it, or those that smell to it, they shall say the truth by and by."

* fleas, bedbugs

Merry Pranks

Then went the Jews to counsel what was best to be done. Then said the oldest Jew of them all, "Me think it is best and most expedient for us to buy that merchandise, for then shall we know when that our Messias shall come. Therefore I counsel you to buy it, for it shall be to us a great jewel and comfort," and continently they were agreed all for to buy the merchandise of Eulenspiegel.

And then they returned with right great haste unto Eulenspiegel. And when they were come, they asked the price of one of the prophets that was wrapped in the silk. Then answered Eulenspiegel to the Jews, "Depart from hence, and let my merchandise alone, for it is to costly for you to buy, for one of them shall cost you five hundred gold guldens, and ye will have it. Then answered the Jews to Eulenspiegel and said, "The price is all too great for us." Then said, he, "That I told you before, and therefore if thou will not buy, then depart shortly from hence." And then the Jews, hearing Eulenspiegel speak so sharply to them and make no more count unto them, then they believed him, and continently they gave to him five hundred gold guldens without speaking of any more words, for he spake so angrily that they were afraid to displease him.

And when they had bought it, they brought it to the principal Jew, and they caused him to aggregate all the Jews both old and young. When they were assembled, then he said that by the might of God they had got a prophet, and he said, "He that should have it in his mouth should prophesy the truth." And then he said to the Jews, "By this prophet, we shall know when our Messias shall come," and he commanded them to fast three days; and then he, Isaac, should take it in his mouth and prophesy the truth, and so he did. And as he had it in his mouth, and another Isaac asked it him how it savored, and he answered, "I am inspired with the holy ghost to prophesy the truth. There must be another of God's servants to have it in his mouth," and so he did.

When he had tasted thereof, he said, "I am inspired with the holy ghost. I shall tell you the truth. We are beguiled, for it is no other thing but a turd." And they tasted, and the turd hanged in their teeth with the hair that he had cut from his arse, and then they knew well that they were deceived.

And forthwith departed Eulenspiegel from thence, and he went toward his own country and made good cheer with good fellows homeward, as long as the money would last.

How Eulenspiegel had gotten the parson's horse, by his confession

In Kyssenburg in that village was a parson that had a fair horse and a proper handmaiden, which he loved one as the other. Then it fortuned that the duke of Brunswick on a time saw the horse, and when that he had seen the horse, his mind ran so much on the horse that he must needs have him. Then upon a time came the duke and desired the horse oftentimes of the parson, and the parson said him, nay. Then was the duke sorry because he might not have the horse, and he durst not take by force, for he was one of the council of Brunswick.

And when Eulenspiegel heard that the duke desired the horse, then said Eulenspiegel to the duke, "An you will reward me, I shall get you the parson's horse." Then answered the duke to Eulenspiegel, "I shall give thee my gown of red chamblot the one sleeve set with pearls." Then said Eulenspiegel to the duke, "I shall bring him. I have no doubt." So departed Eulenspiegel, and he came to the inn, where he was well known, and the host said he was welcome. And Eulenspiegel rested there three days, and after that he made himself sick.

Then was he brought to bed sick that* the parson of the town and his maid were so heavy and knew not how to do nor him to help. And then began he to wax sicker and sicker. And then said the parson to Eulenspiegel, "I counsel you to be shriven and to take your rites of the holy church, as it belongeth to a true Christian man." And when Eulenspiegel heard the parson speak to him, then said Eulenspiegel to the parson, "I desire you heartfully to be confessed, for I know myself guilty and a great sinner." Then the parson examined him under confession right busily, he bade him to remember that he had a soul for to keep, and he preached and teached to him the use of confession. And then showed Eulenspiegel to him part of his mind, and at the last, when he spake no more, then asked the parson of Eulenspiegel if that he had no more sins in his mind that were great and abominable, that he was ashamed to show.

Then answered Eulenspiegel to the parson, "Yes, I have one more, and that I dare not confess me of to you, and therefore, you must fetch me another priest, for if I

---
* so that

should show it unto you, then would ye be angry and out of patience." Then answered the parson to Eulenspiegel and said, "The way is far from this place and very foul. Moreover, if it fortuned you in the meanwhile to die, then were we both in great peril and danger. And therefore tell me that sin, and I shall absolve ye thereof, be it never so great and abominable. And if I were angry with you, yet you know I must keep your counsel. And if it be any thing that longs to me, I forgive ye freely, and therefore tell it me." Then longed he more then ever he did.

Then said Eulenspiegel to the priest, "I know well that you will be angry, but I feel me sore sick that I ween* that I shall die, and therefore I shall show it to you quickly." And then he said, "I have lain by your maid, your servant." Then asked he, "How oft have ye lain by her?" And then said Eulenspiegel, "No more then five times." And then the

* think

priest thought in his mind, therefore the devil break thy neck, and he gave him absolution shortly, and forthwith he departed from Eulenspiegel to his house.

And when he came home, he called his maid to him and asked if she had lain by him. And the maid answered to him and said, "That did I never." Then answered the priest, "Thou liest, for under confession he hath told me that he hath lain by thee more than five times." And then the maid said nay and the priest yes, and then the priest took a staff in his hand and he beat is maid therewith, that she was both black and blue.

And Eulenspiegel lay in his bed and laughed, and in the morning waxed Eulenspiegel whole and arose and said it was well amended with him, and he asked his hostess and the priest what he had spend in his sickness. And then reckoned the priest, he knew not what, for he was so angry in his mind, and the maid also, for she was beat for his sake. And then said Eulenspiegel, "Tell me what is my duty to pay?" And the priest answered not a word, and then said Eulenspiegel to him, "Remember you not, master parson, that you have disclosed my confession? I shall ride to Halberstat to the bishop, and I shall complain on you that you descried my confession that I confessed me unto you."

When the priest hard Eulenspiegel speak after that manner, then forgot he his anger and fell on his knees before him, for he thought that he was in more danger then ever he was before, and then he said to Eulenspiegel, "If that you will keep your peace and make no more words hereof, I shall give to you twenty gold guldens, and I shall do as much for you as lies in me for to be done."

Then made Eulenspiegel himself very angry with the parson, and said unto him, "If that you would give me an hundred gold guldens that I should not show, I will not take them for my gown."

Then the priest prayed the maid with weeping tears,

that she would go to Eulenspiegel and to entreat him that he should not go to show the Bishop, and bid him ask what he will and he shall have it. Then went the maid to Eulenspiegel, and she showed him what the priest said, and then came Eulenspiegel to the priest and said, "Will you give to me your horse that you love so well, and then shall I keep your counsel. And I tell you plainly, I will have no other thing than that only." And then the priest was more sorry than ever he was, and he said to Eulenspiegel that he would give to him as much money as he would desire and not to ask his horse. Then said Eulenspiegel, "I will have none other thing but only the horse," and then the parson had liever lose his horse than he would have the bishop to know. Then gave he the horse to Eulenspiegel with ill will.

And then when Eulenspiegel had the horse, then he departed from the parson and was very glad. And then he came toward the duke, And when he was come there, the duke spied Eulenspiegel and the parson's horse; then was he very glad, And then brought Eulenspiegel the horse to him, whereof he was very glad, and then gave he the gown of red chamblot to Eulenspiegel, and he thanked him greatly for that gift and laughed. And the priest was very angry for the loss of his horse, and oftentimes he beat his maiden therefore, for he said, she was the cause thereof. And he beat his maid so oft, that at the last she ran from him, and so he lost both his horse and the maid. And the priest loured on* Eulenspiegel ever after, that loved him so well before,

How Eulenspiegel was hired of a blacksmith

In Rostock in Mecklenburg dwelleth a smith that hired Eulenspiegel for his man, and when he was hired, he put him to the bellows to blow. And when he blew not well, then took the smith the bellows in his hand and blew and

* looked angrily at

said, "Fellow, do thus. Bear the bellows upright," and then he gave the bellows to Eulenspiegel again, then went the smith forth with into the garden.

And then took Eulenspiegel the bellows on his neck and followed after his master with them into the garden, where his master was a shitting, and then said Eulenspiegel to his master, "Where shall I leave this bellows that I may go fetch the other unto you?" Then answered his master and said, "Good man, what meanest thou? Art ye not well in thy mind? Go take the bellows and bare them where thou had them."

He spake fair to Eulenspiegel and right loath he was to displease him, for every night by the space of eight days long he called up every night his servants at midnight for to work, whereof they marveled what he meant, for they were very angry therewith, and one said to the other, "I think our master is not well in his mind that he rises every night at

midnight to work. He was not wont so for to do in times past." And as they were speaking of this rising together, then said Eulenspiegel to his fellows and asked them if that they would be well content with him and if he asked of his master what was the cause that he did call them up every night at midnight to work. And then answered the servants, "We will not be displeased therewith, but right glad thereof, and well content therewith." And then said Eulenspiegel to the servants, "I will go to him." And forthwith spake Eulenspiegel to his master and said to him, "Wherefore do ye wake us every night at midnight out of our sleep?" Then answered the smith and said, "That is my manner, that my men the first eight days suffer I not them to sleep but half the night."

Then held Eulenspiegel his peace, and all his fellows, and said no more words, and the next night the smith called his men at midnight to work. And Eulenspiegel then took the bed and bare it on his back, and when the iron was hot, the master beat it so hard that the sparks flew on the bed of Eulenspiegel. Then said his master, "Will not that ungracious fellow arise?" Then came Eulenspiegel with his bed on his back. And when the master saw the bed on his back, he said "What wilt thou do with the bed? Bear it into the place where thou had it." Then answered Eulenspiegel to his master, "Be ye not angry with me, for this is my manner ever. For when that I have slept the one half of the night, then bear I the bed on my back the other half of the night" Then began the smith to wax angry and said, "Go bear the bed where thou had it, and then go thou above out of my house." Then answered Eulenspiegel and said "Master, with a good will," and then he bare the bed up into the place where it was before. Then when he had borne the bed in his place, then took he a ladder and climbed up to the house top, and there he brake a great hole in the house top, and pulled away the thatching thereof, and he passed through and went over the houses, and so went his way from thence and never came thereafter.

And as the smith was busy working, they heard a great noise above in the chamber and a great knocking, Then asked he his servants, who was above in the chamber that made such a noise. Then answered the men to their master and said, "We know not who is above." Then said the smith, "Then will I go look," and then left the smith his work and went up into the chamber, and when he was above, he saw all the roof of the chamber was pulled down and also cast all about. Then was he angry and wist not what to do, for he wist not who had done it. And at the last he looked up and spied the ladder. Then knew he well that it was Eulenspiegel's deed. Then came he down and fetched a sword, and he would have run after him to have slain him. Then the servants, seeing the master taking the sword, they held him and asked him what he would do. Then answered he and told how Eulenspiegel had done. The answered the servants to their master, "Let him go, for he hath done as you bade him, for you bade him go upon the house, and so he hath done, as ye may see."

And so the smith was content, and then he caused his house to be new thatched again.

How Eulenspiegel was hired of a shoemaker

Upon a time served Eulenspiegel a shoemaker, and upon a time, the shoemaker had business in the town, and then gave he to Eulenspiegel a hide of leather, and bade him that he should cut all the hide. And Eulenspiegel asked him what fashion he should cut them, and the master said, "Little and great, as the swineherd did drive his beasts." And then said Eulenspiegel, "With a good will."

And then departed the cordinner,* and then took Eulenspiegel the hide and began to cut the leather for oxen and sheep's feet, and swine. Then came his master home and came to see what his servant had cut out and to look whether he had cut the leather as he bade him. And when that he had seen that he had cut out his leather all in beasts' claws then was he angry and said to Eulenspiegel, "Wherefore hast thou marred all my leather and cut it for beasts' feet?" Then answered he to him and said, "I have done as ye bade me." The master said, "Thou liest, for I bade thee that thou should not mar my leather." Then answered Eulenspiegel to his master and said, "I have done as ye bade me. Ye bade me that I should cut both great and small, as the swineherd driveth out his beasts, and that have I done." Then answered the cordinner to Eulenspiegel and said, "I meant not that. I meant that ye should have cut out of the

* a shoemaker or worker in cordovan leather

hide both great shoon and little shoon." Then answered Eulenspiegel to his master, "If that ye had told me it before, I would have done it with a good will. And I pray you master forgive me this, and I shall now do it with a good will." And then did his master forgive him for that time, and then promised Eulenspiegel to his master that he would do that that he bade him.

Then the next day after, cut Eulenspiegel's master himself the shoon out both little and great, and gave them to him, and he bade him that he should sew the great with the small, and Eulenspiegel said, "With a good will." And then took Eulenspiegel the shoon, and put the little shoon into the great shoon, and sewed them both together, as his master bade him, and that spied his master and said, "Ye be a good servant, for ye do all thing that I bid you." Then answered Eulenspiegel and said, "They that do as they be bid, they be worthy to have thank." Then said the master, "Ye do after my saying and not after my meaning, for I mean that first ye should have sewed a little pair and after a great pair."

And the master was hasty and took him other leather and said, "Cut me all this leather upon one last." And the master thought no more of the falseness of Eulenspiegel, and he departed to his chamber, and when he was come home, then remembered he what he had said to Eulenspiegel. Then went he as fast as he could toward the shop where as Eulenspiegel was, and when he came there Eulenspiegel had cut all the leather upon the little last, all for the left foot. Then when his master saw all his leather cut for the left foot, then asked he Eulenspiegel if there belonged not to they left foot a right foot, and he was very angry with him. Then said Eulenspiegel to his master, "If that ye had told to me before, I would have cut them, but an it please you, I shall cut as many right shoon unto them." The master said, "I bade ye cut the one with the other," and then answered Eulenspiegel, "Ye bade me cut all upon one last."

Then answered the shoemaker, "If that I should keep you long, you would make me so poor that I must needs go a begging, but now give me money for my leather that thou hast marred me, and depart thou from hence." Then answered Eulenspiegel to the shoemaker, "The hide of a bull will make two hides," and with those words he arose and said, "In this house have I been, but I will not come here again," and so departed he from thence.

How Eulenspiegel sold turds for fat

And as Eulenspiegel had destroyed much leather of the shoemaker, whereof the shoemaker was very sorry, and that hearing, Eulenspiegel returned again to the town and came to his master and told him that he had a last of tallow, and he told his master that he should have it good cheap, for to restore him part of the harm that he had done to him before in his leather. And then the shoemaker said, "If it be good, I pray you, let me have it before another," and then said Eulenspiegel, "With a good will."

And then departed they, and then went Eulenspiegel to the turds fermer and made him fill twelve barrels with turds for a little money, and then took he a little tallow and put in the barrels four inches thick, as though it had been altogether grease, and closed it so close that it could not stink, for it was in the winter when there was a great frost that the dirt was fast frozen to the barrel. And the other six barrels he filled with other tallow or fat more thicker than the other six were, for they were the example of his merchandise. And when that he had dressed all the barrels, he send for his master the shoemaker, and he asked him if that he would come to see the merchandise, and he said he would.

Then within a while came the shoemaker to Eulenspiegel, and when he was come there, Eulenspiegel made the heads of the best barrels to be broken up. When the cordener saw

the barrels, they liked him very well. And then Eulenspiegel asked him how the barrels pleased him, and he answered "Very well," and then asked he the price, and then answered Eulenspiegel, "Ye shall give me no more then four and twenty guldens, twelve in hand and the other twelve at the year's end. And then was the shoemaker content, and thought no deceit, and gave to him twelve guldens in hand. And Eulenspiegel received the money, and then departed he.

And the cordinner was glad of the bargain and thought that the foresaid harm that he had done him should be restored. And then he hired a servant to melt the tallow, and he brought one barrel by the fire, and when the dirt began to wax hot, it began to smell. Then said the one to the other, I ween some of us hath beshitten their breeches. And then came the master and bade them make clean their shoon, for one of you hath trodden in a turd, and then they looked about, but they found nothing. And then should they have put one of they barrels in the cauldron, then saw they well that it was the barrel that stank, for it was full of turds.

And then they left their work and went for to seek Eulenspiegel, but he was gone, and so the shoemaker must suffer the last loss with the first.

How Eulenspiegel served a tailor

On a time served Eulenspiegel a tailor, and the tailor asked him if that he could sew well a cloth that no man might see the seam. And then said Eulenspiegel, "Yes."

And then went Eulenspiegel and sewed under a barrel. Then said his master, "What dost thou now? This is a marvelous sewing." Then answered Eulenspiegel, "I sew so close that no man can see, as you bade me, nor I myself see not." Then answered his master, "Good servant, I meant not so. I bade thee sew that every man might see."

And then the third night the master had labored so sore that he must needs sleep. Then cast he to Eulenspiegel a husbandman's gown, and he bade him take a wolf and make it up. And then said Eulenspiegel, "I shall do it." Then went he to bed. Then cut Eulenspiegel the husbandman's gown and made thereof a wolf with the head and feet. And when that he had sewed it together, then set he it upon the table with staves. Then in the morning arose his master and came down, and when he saw the wolf standing upon the table, he was afraid and asked him what he had done. And he said, "Master, I have made a wolf as you bade me." Then said the master, "I meant that you should have made up the russet gown, for a husbandman's gown is called here a wolf." Then answered Eulenspiegel, "If that I had known that before, I would have done so, for I had liever have done a gown than a wolf," and at the last was the master content.

And within four days after, watched* the master so much that he must needs go to sleep, and there was a coat ready made, but it lacked the sleeves. Then the master took the coat and the sleeves and gave them to Eulenspiegel, and he bade him that he should cast on the sleeves, and he said he would. Then went his master to bed, and then took Eulenspiegel the coat and hanged it on a balk and set on every side a candle, and stood up and cast the sleeves at the coat all the night long. And then arose the tailor and spied Eulenspiegel, and he cast the sleeves more faster then ever he did before at the coat. And that spied well the tailor and said, "What foolish touches be those that you do there?" And then answered Eulenspiegel very angrily, "This is no foolish touch, for I have stand all the night casting the sleeves at the coat, and they will not abide thereon, and now I see it is but lost labor." Then said the master to Eulenspiegel. "It is

* stayed awake

my fault, for I weened that he would have understand me better, for I meant you should have sewed on the sleeves on the coat."

Then said Eulenspiegel to his master, "The devil take you, for if ye had said so to me before, I might have sewed on the sleeves and have gone to sleep. But now, master, go you and sew all the day long, and I will go sleep." And then answered the tailor, "And have I hired you to sleep?" And thus began they to chide, and as the were thus chiding, the tailor bade him pay for his candles that he had burned that night, and then Eulenspiegel spake never a word more but took all his clothes and went his way and came no more there.

How Eulenspiegel through his subtle deceits deceived a wine drawer in Lubeck

On a time came Eulenspiegel to Lubeck, where is very strait Justice, and the while that Eulenspiegel was there abiding, he heard tell of a wine drawer that was in a lord's cellar that was very proud and presumptuous. And it was said that there was no man that could deceive him nor pass him in wisdom, and there was none of all the lords that loved him. Then thought Eulenspiegel in his mind how he might deceive him.

Then upon a time took Eulenspiegel two pots, one of water and the other empty, and he hid the pot of water that no man saw it, and he came to the cellar, and gave the wine drawer the empty pot, and bade him fill the pot with wine, and so he did. And when it was full, he brought it up to Eulenspiegel, and then he looked aside, and in the mean while Eulenspiegel set the pot of water in the place of wine and hid the pot of wine. And then asked he the wine drawer what he should pay. And the drawer said, "Ten miten."* Then said Eulenspiegel,

---

* mites, small coins

"The wine is too dear for me. I have but eight miten." Then was the drawer angry and said "Will ye set another price on the wine then the lords have set?" Then said Eulenspiegel, "I have no more money, and I shall not have it so. Then take your wine again, for I knew it not before." Then was the wine drawer very angry, and he took the pot with the water, and bare it down into the cellar and poured out the water into the vessel, and he weened it had been the wine and came and gave Eulenspiegel the pot and said, "Make ye me fill wine and ye have no money to pay for it? Ye ween ye be a fool?" And then said Eulenspiegel, "Ye be beguiled of a fool," and with that word he went his way with the pots.

And then the drawer, mistrusting Eulenspiegel for the words that he said, took a sergeant and overtook him and searched him, and then they found that he had two pots under the mantel.* Then took they Eulenspiegel and peached†

* cloak
† impeached

him for a thief and brought him to the prison. And then said some that he had deserved to be hanged, and some said that it was done for the nonce* to deceive the wine drawer and that was but well done, for he should have seen thereto before, for he said daily that no man should beguile him. But they that loved not Eulenspiegel said that he was a thief and that he should be hanged, and then was Eulenspiegel brought before the judge, and he gave sentence that he should be hanged. And on the morrow was he brought unto the gallows for to be hanged, for they that loved him not would fain have seen justice done on him, and there were gathered many of the town to see Eulenspiegel suffer death. But the lords of Lubeck were sorry for him, for some weened that he could do witchcraft that he thereby might be delivered. And as he was led toward the gallows, he lay all still as though he had been dead. And when he came under the gallows, then desired he to speak with the lords. And when the lords were come, he fell upon his knees and he prayed them that they would grant him a boon, and the lords said, "Thou wouldst desire thy pardon." Then said Eulenspiegel that would I not ask life nor money, nor it shall not cost you one penny. Then all the lords of Lubeck went to the other side of the gallows, and there they laid their heads together, and there they rehearsed his words again, and they agreed to grant him his petition. That done, they came to him and they bade him ask what he would, save those words spoken of before to be except.

And Eulenspiegel thanked the lords and said, "I pray you that every one of you give me your hands so thereof." And they all together gave him their hands, so that all the lords had granted him both with word and hand. Then said Eulenspiegel to the lords, "Because I know you be faithful of your words, I shall show to you my boon." And then he said, "This is my boon. Then every lord of Lubeck do come

---

* for the particular purpose

and kiss my arse when that I have hanged on the gallows by the space of three days long, with his mouth, in the morning fasting, and the borough master first and all the lords after in order." Then answered the lords to Eulenspiegel and said that his desire was an unmannerly boon for to be asked. And then said Eulenspiegel to the lords of Lubeck, "I know the council of Lubeck, that they will hold that that they have promised me both with hand and mouth." Then went the lords again to council; then said they one to the other, "This thing that he asketh of us is unlawfully asked, for it were a great shame for us all that we that be the greatest lords of the town should come and kiss his arse. Better it were for to give him his pardon and let him go his way, for it is but a small fault that he hath done." Then agreed all they lords and said that it was best so for to do. Then the lords called the sergeants, and they bade them too unbind Eulenspiegel and to let him go at large, for all they had granted him his pardon. And then they unloosed Eulenspiegel.

And when Eulenspiegel was at large, he thanked the lords. And then departed he from Lubeck and never came there after.

How Eulenspiegel became a maker of spectacles who could find no work

On a time, the senators of Rome[*] had great discord among themself, which of all the lords should be emperor. And at the last was the earl of Supplenburg king of Romans and emperor of Rome, but there were many other that looked for it. So when he was made, he lay six weeks long before the town of Frankfurt, abiding there for all other lords to torment where was great company assembled.

---

[*] The electors who choose the emperor of the Holy Roman Empire, not the senators of ancient Rome.

And this hearing Eulenspiegel, he thought in his mind to go thither, and so he did, and there bethought to get some gift, an it were no more but the emperor's silver harness. And as Eulenspiegel passed by Frankfurt, he met with the bishop of Trier, and he asked him what he was. Then answered Eulenspiegel, "I am a spectacle maker came out of Brabant, and I can find no work. Then said the Bishop, "Me think your craft should be better daily, for the people the longer they live, they less sight they have. Therefore your craft should be the better." And then said Eulenspiegel to the bishop, "My lord, you say truth, but there is one thing that destroy our craft, and if you will take no displeasure, I shall show it to you." And then the Bishop bade him say what he would. And then said he, "This destroyeth our craft, that such great lords as you be kings, dukes, earls, lords, bishops, knights, lawyers and governors of lands and towns, all those look through their fingers and not with

spectacles. They were wont to study in the old time the right,* and then behooved the men many spectacles. And also the priests were wont to study and read their service, but now they use no spectacles at all. And by this manner is our craft destroyed and naught set by. And by heads of the country that poor men of the country learn all to look through their hands that they be almost as cunning as the heads of the country."

Then the bishop understood the text but not the gloss, and he spake to Eulenspiegel and said, "Come with me to Frankfurt, and I shall give unto thee my harness or clothing." And then was Eulenspiegel very glad, and he went with the bishop to Frankfurt where the emperor was chosen. And when the triumph was done, then the bishop gave him that that he promised him, and then was he glad and he went with the bishop, and so he returned again to Saxony.

How Eulenspiegel was hired of a merchant to be his cook

At Mildesheim dwelled a merchant that on a time went walking without the town, and as he walked he found Eulenspiegel lying on a green hill. Then asked the merchant Eulenspiegel what he was. Eulenspiegel answered under his covered falseness, "I am a cook and without a master." Then said the merchant, "If you will be a good servant, I will hire you, and give unto you wages. I have a cook at home, but my wife complaineth on him alway." Then promised Eulenspiegel the merchant to be true to him.

Then asked the merchant his name. Then answered Eulenspiegel, "My name is Bartholomeus." Then said the merchant, "That name is all too long. Your name shall be Dole." Then said Eulenspiegel, "I hold me contented therewith."

* law

Then said the merchant, "Dole, my man, now let us go gather some herbs for young chickens, for tomorrow I must have guests to dinner." And then went they home to his place together, and when the merchant's wife saw Eulenspiegel, she asked her husband, "What shall we do with this man? Ween you that our bread moulds?" Then said the merchant, "Be content wife. This shall be your man, for he is a cook."

Then called he his man and said, "Dole, take a basket and follow me to the flesh shambles,"* and so he did. And when they were there, the merchant bought meat for to roast, and when he came home, he called his man and said, "Dole, tomorrow lay the meat to the fire, and roast it coldly that ye burn it not." And Eulenspiegel said he would, and then he arose in the morning and brought the meat by the fire, and he took the meat that he should roast and put it on the spit and bare it down into the cellar, and he laid it between two barrels of beer, that it should lie cold enough and burn not. And because the merchant should have guests, he came home before to see whether that his meat was well roasted or not. And when he came home, he called Dole and asked him if that the meat was ready, and Eulenspiegel answered, "The master shall see the roasting."

"Where hast thou done it?"

"Beneath in the cellar between two barrels, for in all the house could I not find so cold a place to lay it in for burning."

The merchant said, "Is it not roasted?" And Eulenspiegel said, "Nay, for I did as ye bade me. I laid it cold enough, for I know not the time that you would have had it roasted."

And as they were talking together came in the guests, and the merchant told to his guests how that Eulenspiegel had served him, and they laughed threat. But his wife was not content therewith, and right glad she would have been rid of him, and very angry she was because of that touch.

* meat market

Then said the merchant to his wife, "Be contented at this time, for tomorrow I must to Gosslir, and he shall wait on me, and when I shall come home again, then shall I put him away from hence."

And then went the merchant with his guests to dinner and made good cheer, and at night called the merchant his man and said, "Dole, make the wagon ready, for tomorrow I am in thought that I and my priest take our journey to Gosslir, and grease it that it may go trim." And then went Eulenspiegel and greased the wagon within and without, and in the morning went the merchant and the priest to the wagon and rode their way, and by the way, the priest laid his hand on the rails of the cart, and they made his hands all grease, and then he looked better and both the merchant and the priest were all arrayed with grease. Then they called Eulenspiegel, and they bade him see, and very angry they were with him, and in the mean time came there a man of the country with a load of straw, and then they bought part of his straw and dressed their wagon therewith for shielding of their clothes, and then they went unto the wagon again.

Then said the merchant angrily, "Go drive it under the gallows," and as he was a little further, he spied a gallows, and thither drove he the wagon under the gallows, and when it was under the gallows, he made the wagon to stand still and he untied the horse. Then said the merchant, "What will you now do?" Then said Eulenspiegel, "Tarry you here all night, for you bade me to drive you under the gallows." And when they saw that they were under the gallows, the priest laughed but the merchant was very angered and bade him to drive forthright and never to stand still. Then said Eulenspiegel he would. Then pulled he out a pin that was in the wagon that held it fast to the horse and drove the horse forth and he left them under the gallows. Then the merchant seeing that, he leapt out of the wagon and the priest with him, and they ran after him, and at the last they overtook

him. And then the merchant drew his sword and would have smite him, but the priest would not suffer him. And then made he fast the horse again and so drove the journey to an end.

When the merchant was come home, his wife asked how he fared and how he liked his man. He answered, "Not of the best." Then he called Eulenspiegel, and he bade him tarry there that night, and in the morning to depart from thence, for he said he was but a beguiler and a deceiver wheresoever he went. Then said Eulenspiegel, "Good master, that shall I do."

And then arose Eulenspiegel early in the morning, and as he was up the merchant said, "Eat and drink your belly full, and rid the house of you that I find you not here when that I come again, for I must to church, and when I return, if I find you here, stand to that that shall befall," And Eulenspiegel held his peace and spake never a word to him, and then the merchant went to church. Then he began for to rid all the household stuff and bear it into the street. Then came word unto his master to the church that all his household stuff stood in the street. Then came the merchant home and saw that it was Eulenspiegel that had borne out all his stuff. He asked his man why he did so, and Eulenspiegel said, "I did as you bade me, for ye bade me that I should rid your house, and so I have of all your stuff that ye have."

Then said the merchant to Eulenspiegel, "Depart from hence and come no more here. I give thee warning, for here is nobody that thanks thee for thy labor." And then departed Eulenspiegel his way, and so was the merchant fain to carry in his gear again that Eulenspiegel had borne out.

How Eulenspiegel was desired to dinner

In Lunenburg dwelled a flute maker that knew vagabonds by sight, and on a time it fortuned him to spy Eulenspiegel, to whom he said, "Tomorrow I desire you to dine with me." Then Eulenspiegel thanked him and said that he would.

And then departed the flute maker, and on the morrow at noon, Eulenspiegel went to the pipe maker's house, and when he was there, the doors were shut. And he tarried till noon was past, and then he knew well that he was greatly deceived, and so he returned home again.

And on the morning as he walked in the market, he spied the pipe maker, and then went he to him and thanked him for his dinner, and he said "When ye bid a body to dinner, ye shut all your doors." And the pipe maker said, "I bade you come to dinner." Then said Eulenspiegel, "Your doors were shut." Then laughed the pipe maker and said, "Go to my house before, and I shall come after to dinner, for ye shall find both roast and sodden." And then departed Eulenspiegel to the pipe maker's house, and there he found all true as the pipe maker had told him.

And then said he to the pipe maker's wife that she

should go as fast as she could to her husband, for he said that he had a great sturgeon given him, and he said that he would turn the spit till that she came again. The woman said, "Good Eulenspiegel, keep the house till that I come again, and let no body in." Then departed the woman with her maid towards her husband as fast as she could and met with him by the way, and when he saw her, he asked her whither she went so fast. And she said to help him. For she said that Eulenspiegel had told her that ye had a sturgeon given you, and he said that ye bade that we should come and help you for it was so great that you were not able to bear it. Then was the man angry and said, "Know ye not well that Eulenspiegel is such a mocker and a deceiver." Then went he home with his wife, and when he came home he knocked at the door, and Eulenspiegel said, "Let be your knocking, for the host hath charged me, that I should let no guest in till dinner was done." Then went the host to his neighbors and tarried there till Eulenspiegel had dined. And when

Eulenspiegel had dined, then he opened the door, and then the pipe maker came with all his folk. And when he was within, he said to Eulenspiegel that it was no honesty for a guest to shut his hostess out of the doors.

And in this manner, he served the host and his hostess.

How Eulenspiegel won a piece of cloth of a man of the country

Eulenspiegel would ever fare well and make good cheer, but he would not work. Then on a time came he to Olssem, to a goodly company of men of the country, and as he walked he espied one man alone with a green cloth on his arm. Then imagined he in his mind how that he might get the cloth, so he came to him, and he asked him where he was dwelling, and then the husband told him, and then departed Eulenspiegel from him, and continently he met with a Scottish priest and another knave, and he said to them, "I desire you to help me, and I shall give you for your labor," and they said they would. Then said Eulenspiegel, "When I call you to record to know what color yonder cloth is, ye shall say blue. I will go before and come after."

Then went he to the husbandman, and he asked him how he sold his blue cloth. Then said the husbandman that it was green and not blue. "I hold twenty guldens against thy cloth that it is blue." Then said the husbandman, "I hold you."

"It is done," said Eulenspiegel, "and the first man that comes hereby shall be the judge thereto."

"Agreed," said the husbandman.

And then made Eulenspiegel a sign to the men that he had hired, and they come. Then said the husbandman, "We two strive what color this cloth is. I pray you break our strife." Then the fellow said, "It is fair blue cloth." Then said the husbandman, "Ye be too false for me to meddle with, for it is made betwixt you two to deceive me." Then

said Eulenspiegel, "Cause that ye saieth we be agreed, let him go. Here cometh a priest. Will ye be contented what he saieth?" And the man of the country said yes. Then came the priest by. Then said Eulenspiegel, "I pray you to tell us what color this cloth is." The priest said, "Ye see well enough. What need you to ask me?" The husbandman said, "I know the color of this cloth well enough, but these two men say it is another color, and therefore we strive." Then said the priest, "What have I to do with your striving?" Then said the husbandman, "I pray you, sir, depart us of our striving." Then said the priest, "I can see no other but that it is a fair blue." And then said the husbandman, "An ye were not a priest, in faith ye did lie, for there be three false men. But sith ye be a priest, I must believe you." And then gave he Eulenspiegel the cloth, and went his way.

Then did Eulenspiegel with his two fellows clothe them with the husbandman's cloth against the winter. But the good poor man prayed to God many a time and oft that the devil might take them al three, for the poor man was the worse all the days of his life after that great loss.

How Eulenspiegel gave twenty guldens to twelve poor men for Christ's love

On a time came Eulenspiegel to Hanover, where he did many virtuous things. On a time, rode Eulenspiegel without the town, and as he rode he met with twelve blind men to whom he said, "Whither will ye go?" The blind men so hearing that he was on horseback, they put off their caps, for they weened that he had been a great gentleman, and said, "We have been at a dole of a rich man that died yesterday in the town." Then said Eulenspiegel, "I take great thought for you how you shall do this winter, for me think you shall freeze to death before the winter be done." And then he said, "Hold, here is twenty guldens, and return again all you to the place where that I was lodged," and he named his host, and he bade them make good cheer till winter were done. And then they thanked him, for they thought that he had give them money, but he did not.

And then departed they to the place whither he sent them, and they thought that some of the company had the money. And when that they came to the inn, they said to the hostess that by the way as they went, they met with a good man that gave them twenty guldens for God's sake, and he bade us come hither and make good cheer, therefore for he said that he had been lodged here, and for this said we should have good cheer. When the host heard that they had money, he took them in and made the good cheer. And when that their twenty guldens were spent, then said the host to them, "Now will you reckon good brethren, for now the twenty guldens be spent." The blind men said, "We be contented to pay you," and then spake one of the blind men and said, "He that hath twenty guldens, pay our host."

And then said the one to the other, "I have not the twenty guldens"; "Nor I have not the twenty guldens" And then some sat and clawed their head, and some clawed their arm, and then they knew that they were deceived. Then thought the host in his mind, "What shall I do with them? Shall I let them go that they spend me no more money? Nay, not so." Then shut he the blind men in the stable and brought to them hay and straw.

And when that Eulenspiegel thought that all the money was spent, then came he riding into the same inn where the blind men were, and he had changed his clothing that they should not know him and so entered into the inn where the blind men were, and led his horse into the stable where the poor men were, and he set up his horse. He came to his host, asked his host wherefore that he had kept the blind men in the stable so fast shut in, and he asked him what harm they had done to him. Then said the host, "I would that they were together in the water so that I had my costs paid me," and then he told him all the matter. And then said Eulenspiegel, "An ye had a borrow, would you let them go," and the host said, "Yes with a good will." Then said Eulenspiegel, "I will go see if I can find any borrow for them."

Then went he to the curate of the church and said, "Master parson, I have an host that this night was take with the fiend. I desire you for to help him." The curate said, "With a good will, but you must tarry two or three days, for it may not be done in haste." "Well," said Eulenspiegel, "that is well said, but I will go fetch his wife that she may hear what you say." And the priest said, "I shall tell to her the same that I told to you without fail." And then went Eulenspiegel home to his host, and he told him that he had found a borrow, and that it was the parson of the church, and let your wife go with me, and she shall hear him speak the same that he hath said to me." And then was the host glad, and he send his wife with Eulenspiegel to the curate. And when they were come to the curate, Eulenspiegel said to him, "Master parson, here is the wife of the man that I spake of to you now. Tell her the same that you have said to me." And the curate said, "With a good will"; then said he to the woman, "Tarry a day or two, and I shall help your husband well." And then was the woman glad and returned home again with Eulenspiegel. And when she came home, she told her husband what the curate said, whereof the host was glad. And he went unto the stable and let the blind men lose and they went their way.

And then Eulenspiegel reckoned with his host and so departed from thence, and when the third day came, then went the woman to the priest, and she asked him twenty guldens that the blind man had spend. The curate asked her, "Hath your husband that ye told* to me?" And the woman said, "No." Then said the curate, "That is the false devil that

---

* what you told me

would have the money." Then said she, "What false devil meanest thou? Give me my money for my costs" Then said the curate to the woman, "It was told me that your husband was taken with the false devil. Bring him hither, and I shall help him thereof, by the grace of God." Then said the woman to the priest, "Such beguilers find I many. Now you should pay me for my costs. You bring to me a back reckoning, and you say my husband is taken with the devil, and that you shall know shortly."

And then she ran to her husband and told him how the priest said to her, and when the host heard those words, he was angry and took the spit with the roast that lay at the fire and ran to the priest's chamber. And when the curate spied him, he was afraid and called the neighbors to help him, and he made a sign of the holy cross before him, and he cried for help to take that man that was so beset with the devil. Then said the host, "Thou, priest, pay me my money," and the priest gave him no answer. Then would the host have run through him with the hot spit, but the neighbors went between them and departed them, and they held the host still with great pain from master parson.

But as long as the host lived, he asked his money of the priest for the costs of the blind men, but the priest answered to him that he owed him naught and naught he would pay him, but said "An you be taken with a devil, I shall help you thereof." But never after loved one the other.

How Eulenspiegel feared his host with a dead wolf

In the Issleuen dwelled an inn holder that was very spiteful and mocking, and he prized greatly his boldness. Upon a time it befell in the winter season, when there had been a great snow, Eulenspiegel came riding with other three merchants from Saxony to the Issleuen, and it was very late when they came there, and when they were come, they entered into the inn that the man kept. Then said their host angrily, "Where have you been so late? It is no time now to take your inn." Then they answered, "Be ye not angry, for we have been hunted with a wolf in the snow. We could not scape till now." Then the host mocked them because they three were hunting of one wolf and said, "If there came ten wolves to me in the field, I would have slain them every one," and mocked the merchants till they went to bed.

And Eulenspiegel sat by the fire, and heard all together then should they go to bed. And it fortuned that Eulenspiegel and the merchants should lie in one chamber. And when they were in the chamber together, they took counsel together how they might stop their host of his mocking. Then said Eulenspiegel, "Our host is full of mocking. Let me alone. I shall pay him well enough that he shall not mock us no more." Then promised the merchants to Eulenspiegel to pay all his costs and give him more money for his labor. Then said Eulenspiegel, "Do your journey and business of your merchandise, and when ye have it, come again and lodge at this inn, and ye shall find me here, and then we shall make our host that he shall mock no more." And then arose the merchants in the morning and called the host and paid him for their costs, and Eulenspiegel also. Then they took their horses and departed from thence. And when they were past a little, he cried to the merchants, "Take heed that the wolf bite you not," in mockage. They thanked their host because he gave them warning before.

And as they rode, Eulenspiegel found a wolf that was frozen to the death, and that he took up, and put in a bag, and laid it before him; and then they returned again to Issleuen, to that inn where they were lodged before. And he kept the wolf so close that no man knew thereof. And when the night was come and that they sat all at supper, then the host began to laugh at them, and he reasoned against their hardiness and against the wolf. Then said they, "So

it fortuned at that time, you said that you would slay ten wolves, but sir first I would see you kill one." And then said the host, "That should I do alone." And thus they jested till they went to bed.

And Eulenspiegel held his peace till that he and the merchants went above all together in the chamber. And then said Eulenspiegel to the merchants, "Friends, let me now begin to work and wake you a little while." And then when the host and all his folk were asleep, then went he privily into the chamber and he fetched the dead wolf that was stiff frozen, and dressed him with stakes, and put two children shoon in his mouth, and made him stand as though he had been alive. And then left he the wolf standing in the hall, and he came again into the chamber to the merchants, and when he was above, he and the merchants called their host. And their host asked them what they would have. Then answered they to him that they would have some drink, for they had so great thirst that they must needs drink; "Let your maid or man bring us some, and we will pay for it tomorrow." Then waxed the host angry and said, "This is the Saxon manner for to drink both day and night." And then he called his maid and bade her that she should give the merchants drink. And then the maid rose, and as she went to light a candle, she saw the wolf with two shoon in his mouth. Then she was afraid and ran to the garden, for she thought that he had eaten both the children.

Then called they again. Then called the host his man and bade him arise and bear the Saxons drink. Then arose he and lighted a candle, for he weened that the maid had slept still. Then looked he aside and saw the wolf stand. He was afraid, and he thought that the wolf had eaten the maid, and let fall the candle and ran into the cellar.

Then called Eulenspiegel and the merchants the third time, and prayed that he himself would bring them some drink, for they said there came no body, or else give them a candle and they would draw it themself. Then arose the host himself, for he weened that his man and his maid were fallen asleep again, and then lighted he a candle, and when that he had done, he looked aside and spied the wolf. And he was so afraid that he fell unto the ground, and then arose he and cried to the merchants, and he prayed them for to come help him, for there was for a wolf that had eaten both his man and his maid. And this heard the maid in the garden and the man in the cellar and come to help their master, and the merchants also.

And Eulenspiegel laughed at this hardy man that would have slain ten wolves and he was made afraid of one dead wolf. And when the host saw it was done in mockage, then was he ashamed, and he wist not what for to say. And then left he his boasting and jesting and went to bed again. And on the morrow, it was known through the town, whereof the host was sore ashamed.

And then in the morning arose the merchants and paid their costs, and Eulenspiegel also, and rode their way. And then never after praised the host his manhood.

How Eulenspiegel flayed a hound and gave the skin for half his dinner

On a time came Eulenspiegel very late into an inn where the host was not at home but only the hostess. This hostess had a bloodhound, the which she loved very well, and as she had nothing to do, she took the hound on her lap and played with him. And Eulenspiegel sat by the fire drinking a pot of beer, and the hostess had taught her hound to drink beer in a dish, and as Eulenspiegel was drinking of his beer, the hound fawned on him and wagged his tail on Eulenspiegel. And then said the hostess, "Give the hound some drink in his dish, for that is the meaning." And Eulenspiegel said, "With a good will," and then gave he the hound often to drink, and he gave him also part of all thing that was on the table, that the hound was full as he might be, and then went he and laid him down stretching him by the fire.

And within a while, Eulenspiegel had eaten enough and then asked the hostess if she would reckon, and she said, "Yes." Then asked he his hostess, if she had had a guest that had eaten her meat and drinketh her drink and should pay nothing, would she be content therewith. Then weened the hostess that he meant himself and thought not of her hound. Then said she to him, "Good friend, here is no man that eateth here but he payeth money or a pledge." Eulenspiegel said, "I am content therewith to pay my part, and the other must pay his part."

And the went the hostess into her chamber for to do her business, and then took Eulenspiegel the hound under his gown, and went unto the stable, and flayed of his skin. And then came he again to his hostess that sat by the fire, and

he had the hound's skin under his gown. And then called Eulenspiegel for a reckoning. When she said the reckoning, he gave her half thereof. Then asked she him who should give to her that other half. Then said Eulenspiegel, "Here is my part. Ye had another guest that went away and paid nothing and ate and drank as well as I did. Let him pay the other half of the money." Then said the hostess, "What guest was that, and what pledge had he to give?" Then said Eulenspiegel, "The best coat that he had on." Then drew he out the dog's skin and said to his hostess, "Here is the best coat that the guest hath." And when she saw her dog's skin, then spake she very angrily and cursedly, "Wherefore have ye flayed my hound?"

Then said Eulenspiegel, "Let alone your banning and your cursing in this manner, for it is your fault, for ye bade to me that I should give to your hound meat and drink, and I told to you that the guest had no money, and ye said that ye would not trust him but that ye would have a pledge or money to pay for his costs, so have I brought to you the best coat that he hath for a pledge."

Then was the hostess more angry and said, "Go out of my house shortly, and never come here more within my doors." Then said Eulenspiegel, "Shall go out of your doors? Nay, but I shall ride out of your doors." Then took he his saddle, and saddled his horse, and light on him, and ere he departed from thence, he said to his hostess, "Keep well your pledge that ye may have your money. And within a while, I shall come unto you unbid, and if I drink not of your drink, then need I not pay nothing." And then departed he from thence and rode his way.

How Eulenspiegel served the same hostess another time, and how he lay on a wheel

Within a while after, came Eulenspiegel to Stassfurt, in the same inn where he had been lodged before, and he had done other clothes on because that his hostess should not know him. And when he was come into the inn, he spied a wheel lie thereby, and then he alighted and came and laid him thereon and bade his hostess good morrow.

And he asked her if she heard any news of Eulenspiegel. And she said, "Nay, what should I hear of him? I cannot suffer him to be named." Eulenspiegel said, "What harm hath he done to you, that ye may not hear speak of him? He is a knave indeed. I never heard tell yet that he came in any place, but ere he departed, he did some shrewd touch." Then said the hostess, "That is true, for it is but seven days agone that, for the great cheer that I made to him, like a traitor he flayed my hound and he gave me the skin for my meat and drink." Then said Eulenspiegel, "That was a knavish touch." And the woman said, "Therefore shall he come to evil end."

Then said Eulenspiegel, "Is this all his reward? It is not

three hours agone sith I saw him lie upon a wheel." Then said the hostess, "Had I known that, I should have beat him with a staff, that I should have broken some of his ribs for that he hath done to me." And then arose Eulenspiegel and said, "Let be your anger, for when I spake to you, he lay upon the wheel. And now, adieu. I come not here again."

How Eulenspiegel set his hostess upon the ashes with her bare arse

As Eulenspiegel was come from Rome, he came to an inn where his host was not at home. And when he was within, he asked his hostess if that she knew not Eulenspiegel, and the hostess said, "Nay, but I hear say that he is a false deceiver and beguiler." Then said Eulenspiegel, "Wherefore say ye so yet know him not?" Then said the hostess, "That is truth, but I have heard speak much of his unhappiness."

Then said Eulenspiegel, "Good woman, he hath done to you never no harm. Wherefore slander ye him for the words of other people?" The hostess said, "I say no other of him than the people do, for I have heard him bespoken of, of many of my guests that have lodged here."

Then held Eulenspiegel his peace and spake no more till in the morning. And then spread he abroad the hot ashes on the hearth, and then took he the hostess out of her sleep and set her thereon on her bare arse, and so was his hostess well burned. Then said he to her, "Now may ye say boldly that ye have seen the false deceiver and beguiler Eulenspiegel." Then cried the hostess for help and loured* upon him.

Then went he out of her doors and said to her, "Should not men correct and reprove slanderers and backbiters, that say it of men and never saw them nor never had done harm to them? Yes, it is a charitable thing to do." And then took he his horse and departed from thence.

* looked angrily

How Eulenspiegel served a Hollander with a roasted apple

Upon a time came Eulenspiegel to Antwerp to an inn where was many Hollanders merry, and he brought with him two eggs which he roasted for to eat, for he was sick and could eat no flesh.

And this seeing, a Hollander said, "The Tom of the country! Will not your hostess meat serve you, but that ye must bring meat with you? Ween ye that ye should have no meat here?" And with those words, he took the eggs and supped them up, and when he had done, he gave to Eulenspiegel the shells and said to him, "Hold, here is the box. The relics be gone," and then laughed all the guests at that touch, and Eulenspiegel also.

And in the evening fetched Eulenspiegel a fair apple, and cut out all the core thereof, and put therein a strong purgation, and roasted the apple in the fire. And then took Eulenspiegel the apple and cut it in pieces upon his trencher, and strewed thereof powder of ginger, and set it upon the table, and went from the table as though he would have gone and fetched more. And as soon as Eulenspiegel had turned his back, the Hollander took the apple and ate it in great haste. And by and by, he fell to parbraking and cast up all that was within him, and he was very sick thereof that the host and all the guests weened that he should have died of the apple.

And then said Eulenspiegel to the guests, "Be not afraid of him, for it is a little purgation that I have given him. He was too hasty to eat the apple soon, or I should have warned him thereof. For the roasted apple could not suffer the eggs in his maw, but that they must needs come out again." And then the guests made good cheer and laughed. And when the purgation had wrought all that it would and that the Hollander was a mended, he said to Eulenspiegel, "Roast and eat whatsoever ye will, for I will never eat with you more."

How Eulenspiegel made a woman that sold earthen pot to smite them all in pieces

Upon a time took Eulenspiegel his journey to Bremen to the bishop, that loved him well for at all times he did some mad touch, whereat he made the bishop to laugh. Then on a time as the bishop and Eulenspiegel were a walking, the bishop desired of him that he would do some merry Jest, but Eulenspiegel went talking to himself, as though he had said his *pater noster*,* and answered not the bishop. But at the last he said to him, "I pray thee to see some news," and he said he would. But he prayed the bishop to tarry a while, and he gave him silence.

And in the meanwhile went Eulenspiegel to a woman that hath earthen pots to sell in the market, the which pots he bought on a condition, that when he made a sign to her, that she should smite all the pots in pieces. And she granted it to him. And then he paid her and returned to the bishop. And when he was come, the bishop asked him where he had been. And Eulenspiegel said, "I was at church."

He said, "My lord, go with me unto the market." And so he did, and when they were there, Eulenspiegel said to the bishop, "See you the woman with the earthen pots? I shall stand here still by you and speak never a word, and yet shall I make her to smite her pots all in pieces. Then said the bishop, "I hold thee thirty guldens that thou shalt not do it," and Eulenspiegel did hold the thirty guldens with the bishop. And then went they into the town house, and there they tarried. And then cried and called the woman, and at the last, made he the sign to her that was made between

---

* The Lord's prayer.

them. And then took she a staff and smite upon the pots so long till that she had broken them every one, so that the bishop and all they that were in the marketplace did laugh thereat.

And as the bishop was come home, then called he Eulenspiegel aside unto him and said, "Tell me shortly what thing ye did to the woman that ye made her take a staff and smite all the pots to pieces, and then shall I give unto you the thirty guldens." Then said Eulenspiegel to the bishop, "My lord, I did it not with sorcery nor witchcraft, but I had paid the woman before for her pots, and we were both agreed." And then laughed the bishop thereat and gave unto Eulenspiegel thirty guldens, and he made him so swear on a book that he should not show nobody the thing, and he said he would give him a fat ox. Then said Eulenspiegel, "That thing shall I do with a good will, and speak never a word." And then departed Eulenspiegel from thence, and he let the bishop do what he would.

And then went the bishop, that when he should make a sign to her, then should she smite the earthen pots all in pieces.* ... as the other did, so that the gift amounted to twenty fat oxen, and then went every man home and fetched a fat ox and brought it unto the bishop.

And when that they were all come in, they stood talking with the bishop and then came Eulenspiegel riding by them, and he saw all the oxen stand there. Then he said unto the bishop, "This gain is half mine." Then said he to Eulenspiegel, "Will you not hold that thing that ye have promised me?" And then said Eulenspiegel, "Yes, for a† fat ox." Then gave the bishop unto Eulenspiegel a fat ox, and he bade him that he should depart, and so he did and left the bishop with all his lords talking.

Then called the bishop all the nobles together, and when that they were come, he said to them, "Now shall I show unto you all this great cunning of the breaking of the pots openly." Then said he to them, "This is it. Eulenspiegel had been before with that woman that sold the earthen pots in the market, and he had paid her for all the pots, and he bade to her that when he should make a sign to her, then should she smite the earthen pots all in pieces, and this was the cunning that Eulenspiegel did."

Then were the nobles ashamed and angry in their mind with the bishop, but they durst not speak one word but clawed their heades when that they saw their fat oxen before their face that they had given to the bishop for that foolish

---

* There is an error in the text. It leaves out a passage saying the bishop played the same trick on the nobles and won twenty oxen from them. Instead, it duplicates the final hundred and one words of this section in this location. This edition removes the duplication to make the text more readable.

† The text says "for another fat ox" rather than "for a fat ox," but that is apparently also an error, since the final sentence says that Eulenspiegel got one of the fat oxen.

deed. But after they comforted themself again and said, "He is our lord and master, and if that he had asked the oxen for naught, we would have given them of him," and Eulenspiegel, for his part got one of the fat oxen, whereof he was glad.

How Eulenspiegel break the stairs that the monks should come down on to matins, and how they fell down into the yard

Eulenspiegel, as he waxed old and feeble and had been in many countries, then began he to take a little repentance on him, and thought to go to be a religious person. Then took he his way to Mariental, and when he came there, he went into the abbey to the abbot. And when he came to him, he desired of the abbot that he might be a brother in the place, and to have a place, he promised the abbot that he would give the abbey all the money that he had.

Then said the abbot to him, and jested with him for he was a merry jester, that he should have a place, but he must have an office therewith for to do some labor as well, that all my brethren do that thing that I command them and take the office that is given unto them, and be content therewith. Then said Eulenspiegel to the abbot, "Whatsoever it please you to bid me do, I shall do it with a good will." Then said the abbot, "The labor is not great that I shall give unto you, for ye shall be porter, so that ye may have conversation with the people daily, and no other thing than for to open the gate and for to shut it again."

Then said Eulenspiegel to the abbot, "God thank you my lord that ye have ordained for me, a poor old man, so light an office, and therefore shall I do all that ye bid me and leave all that ye forbid me." Then said the abbot to him, "Take. Here is the keys. Ye must not let in everybody, nor scarcely in the three nor the four, for there be so many vagabonds and land farers.* For if that ye should let them all in that comes, they would eat and drink so much that at the year's end they would bring the place to a low ebb. Then said Eulenspiegel to the abbot, "That shall I do with a good will."

And then kept he the gate, and when that the servants and monks should have come in, then would he let in no more but the three or the four. And then they complained to the abbot of Eulenspiegel, and told him that Eulenspiegel was a deceiver and a beguiler of folk, for he would not let them in that belonged unto the place. Then called the abbot Eulenspiegel to him and asked him why that he did not let in the servants of the place. And Eulenspiegel answered, "I have done as ye bade me, for ye bade me that I should let in but the third or the fourth and no more, and so I did. And therefore have I not broken your commandment." Then said the abbot, "Ye have done like a false knave, and therefore shall I put ye out of thine office, for ye will not leave your false touches."

And then gave he that office to another monk, and then said he to Eulenspiegel, "This shall be your office. You shall tell† every night how many monks come to matins. An ye miss one, ye shall out of the abbey." Then said Eulenspiegel to the abbot, "My lord, that were I loath for to do, for to go out of the abbey. Well I will do after your commandment." But the abbot gave to him that office because that he would have him out of the abbey, and so for to be rid of him.

And Eulenspiegel thought in his mind not for to tarry long. And then went Eulenspiegel and pulled away two or three steps of the stairs that the monks should come

---

* The text says "landrivers." This edition substitutes "land farers," using an archaic English word for travelers. *Landfahrer* (land traveler) is a German word for vagabond.

† count

down unto matins. And at midnight came the prior first that was a good old man and was wont to be the first; and when he thought to have gone down, he fell and brake his leg. And then he cried piteously, so that the other monks heard him and came running hastily for to see what that he ailed and lacked, and then fell they each after other down the stairs.

Then in the morning complained the monks to the abbot and showed him how that Eulenspiegel had served them. Then was the abbot more angry, and said to Eulenspiegel, "What have ye done?" Eulenspiegel said, "As ye bade me, for ye bade me that I should tell the monks when they came to matins, and so I have done. Look, here is the table."

Then said the abbot, "Go out of the abbey, for ye have told them like a false knave." And then departed Eulenspiegel from that abbey and went to Mölln.

How Eulenspiegel bought cream of the women of the country, that brought it for to sell to Mariental

Within a while after that he would enter into the abbey of Mariental to be a monk, he went a walking on the market day to Bremen, where he saw many women standing there to sell cream. And then went Eulenspiegel to the house where he was lodged, and borrowed a tub of his hostess, and went again into the market. And when he was there, he set down his tub and came to a woman of the country, and he asked the price of her cream. And when they were both agreed, he made her for to put the cream into his tub, and then went he to another and agreed with her also and made her to put her cream into his tub, and so went he from the one to the other till that he had made all the women that had their cream to put it into his tub. And when he had so done, then asked the poor women their money of Eulenspiegel, for they would depart home. Then said Eulenspiegel to the

women, "Ye must do so much for me as to trust me these eight days, for I have no money at this time." Then were the women of the country angry, and they ran to they tub for to take every one of them their cream again, for they would not trust him. And as they would have taken their cream again, then began they to fall together by the ears and said, "Thou takest more then thou should have." And the other stood all weeping and said to them, "Shall I lose my cream?" And other twain were tumbling by the hair in the midst of the canal. And thus they pulled and haled one the other that at the last the tub fell down and arrayed them very foul, so that they were all disfigured and wist not of whom they should be avenged of.

And then arose they and asked, "Where is this false knave that hath brought our milk and hath deceived us so? For had we him here among us, we should christen him here in the cream that is in the canal and paint him therewith as well as we be, for he is a false beguiler and deceiver." But he was gone from thence, for he cast before that such a thing should follow. And when the burgesses of the town and many other folk of the town saw that the canals ran with cream, then went they to the marketplace for to see. And when they were there, they asked how the cream was spilt, and then it was told them. And when that they knew it, then they returned home laughing and praised greatly the falseness and subtlety of Eulenspiegel.

How Eulenspiegel came to a scholar to make verses with him

Eulenspiegel
Mars with scepter and king coronate
Furious in affection, and taketh no regard
By terrible fighting, he is our primate

And god of battle, and person right froward.
Of wars the tutor, the lock, and the ward,
His power, his might, who can them resist?
Not all this world if that himself list.*

The scholar

Not all this world? Who told thee so?
Where is that written? Right fain would I see.
Ye came like a fool, and so shall ye go.
By one person only, deceived ye may be.
And by astronomy, I tell it unto ye.
If that will not help, some shift shall I find,
By craft or cunning, Mars for to blind.

Eulenspiegel

Venus, a god of love most decorate,
The flower of women and lady most pure,
Lovers to concord she doth aggregate
With perfect love as marble so dure.†
The knot of love she knits on them sure
With friendly amity and never to discord
By deeds, thought, cogitation, nor word.

The scholar

Not to discord, yet did I never see
Nor not hear tell of lovers such twain.
But some there was learn this of me,
Either in thought or yet in words plain:
Your reasons be naught. Your tongue goeth in vain.
By natural person, such love is not found
In France, Flanders, nor yet English ground.

Eulenspiegel

The god of wine, that Bacchus hath to name,

---

* wants
† durable, lasting

The sender of fruits, that maketh wines all
My flake, or make or put them in frame,
All at his pleasure and use diurnal,
He may thee exalt and likewise to fall.
Their lord and master and chief governor,
He may them destroy and make in a hour.

The scholar

All to destroy, it is not by his might,
Nor yet for to make, of that be thou sure.
Omnia per ipsum,* Saint John says full right.
Then we call Christ, our God and our treasure.
Presume not so high. You fail of your measure.
Read, hear, and see, and bear well away
Unknown, unsaid, and for grace thou pray.
Vale.†

How Eulenspiegel at Mölln was sick, and how he did shit in the pothecary's‡ boxes, and how he was born in the holy ghost

As Eulenspiegel was come from Mariental, then he fell sick, and when he was sick, he went to Mölln where he was lodged in a pothecary's house for to make medicines therefore. Then should the pothecary give to him a medicine for his sickness, and then he gave to Eulenspiegel a strong purgation. And in the morning the purgation began to work. And then arose Eulenspiegel for to have gone to the draught, but he could not find none, and so he beshit all their chamber. And then he took the twelve boxes that the medicines were in, and he shit in every one of them, and he said, "Here come out the medicines again. It were great pity

---

* All by himself. That is, God alone creates everything, without Bacchus.
† Farewell.
‡ apothecary, druggist

to lose them, for I have no money to give him for them." When the pothecary heard those words, then was he angry. He would have him no longer in his house but took and bare him into an hospital of the holy ghost.

And when he was within, then he said, "I have prayed good long that the holy ghost might come unto me, but my prayer is clean contrary, for I am come into the holy ghost, and he abideth without me, and I in him." Then laughed the people and said, "As men live, so is their end."

Then heard his mother say that he was sick. Then she came to him, and she had thought for to have had some money of him for she was old and poor, and when she saw him, she wept and said, "Where be ye so sick?" And Eulenspiegel said, "Here between the bed and the wall." Then said his mother, "Speak to me one sweet word." Then said Eulenspiegel to his mother, "Honey. Honey, is not that a sweet word?" Then said his mother, "Tell me something that may do me ease." The said Eulenspiegel to his mother, "When that you fartest, turn your arse with the wind, and then you shall feel no stink." Then said his mother, "Give me some of your good." Then said Eulenspiegel to his mother, "He that hath none shall give none, for my good is so secret that no man can find it. An you can find any, take it."

And then Eulenspiegel waxed sicker and sicker so that the folk asked him whether that he would be shriven, for they saw well that he should not recover. Then said an old sister that was a good friend of his, she counseled him to be confessed and take repentance for his sins, and so to be the servant of God. And Eulenspiegel said, "I will not confess me secretly, for all that I have done, I have done it openly to many men in diverse lands; and that is well known, for they that I have done good to, they will say good of me, and they that I have done harm to, they will say harm of me. But I am very sorry of two things the which I could never bring to pass in my life." Then said the sister, "Be sorry of thy sins; and be glad that ye did not those two things, if that they were ill; and if they were good, be sorry because they were not done."

Then said Eulenspiegel, "It is as men will take it, for I was sorry in my mind when I saw a man pick his teeth with his knife, that I had not shitten on the end of it. The other is that I am sorry for, that I did not drive a wooden wedge in all women's arses that were above fifty, for they be neither cleanly nor profitable. I desire it for no other cause but this, that is that they should not shit on the ground, the which bringeth fruits."

Then said the sister to Eulenspiegel, "God save all women of that age and all those that be more. For I hear well, an you were strong and that you had your might as you have had before, you would ere you departed wedge mine arse with a wooden wedge, for I am a woman of sixty years and more." Then he answered to the sister, "I am right sorry and heavy because it is not done." Then answered the sister, "It were much better that the devil had thee." Then answered Eulenspiegel, "It is truth, for a woman is no sooner angry but she is worse than the devil." And then the sister departed and let him lie.

How Eulenspiegel deceived his ghostly* father

And as Eulenspiegel was thus sick, and then they brought to him a priest. And when that priest was come there, he thought in his mind, this hath been a great deceiver of the people and beguiler, wherewith he hath got much money.

And then came the priest unto him and said, "Eulenspiegel remember yourself, for ye have done many sins, and now must you remember that you have a soul to

---

* spiritual

keep, and how you have gotten much money by deceit and falsehood, and now bestow that money to the worship of God and poor priests as I am. And that I counsel you for to do, and I shall order it well and remember you hereafter and do many masses for you." Then said Eulenspiegel, "Good father, if it please you to come at noon again, then shall I make ready some money for you." Then was the priest glad and then departed.

Then took Eulenspiegel an earthen pot and filled it half full of turds, and he strewed thereon a little money, so that the dirt was covered. And when it was noon, the priest came, and he said to Eulenspiegel, "Friend, shall I have that that you promised me?" And Eulenspiegel said, "Yea." Then he set the pot before him and said, "Take now yourself, but be not too hasty nor put not your hand too deep." Then said the priest, "I shall do as you bid me." And Eulenspiegel did open the pot, and he bade the priest to grip softly, for it was almost full. Then was the priest hasty and put his hand into the pot, and he grip a great handful. And when he felt it soft, he pulled out his hand, and it was all beshitten. Then the priest said, "Ye may well be called a deceiver and beguiler, that have deceived his ghostly father, and when ye be at the point of death."

Then said Eulenspiegel to the priest, "Good sir, did I not show unto you before that you should not grip too deep? And if that ye were covetous, it was not my fault."

Then said the priest, "Ye pass in ungraciousness all other that ever I saw. In faith, it was great pity that thou scaped from hanging when thou shouldst have been hanged at Lubeck." And then the priest departed from thence.

Then Eulenspiegel called the priest again, and he said to him, "Master parson, come again, and take your money with you." But he went his way and made it as he heard it not.

How Eulenspiegel made his testament

In the mean time, waxed Eulenspiegel sicker and sicker. Then he called for the lords to make his testament. And when they were come, he gave his goods in three parts: one part to his kinsfolk, another to the lords of Mölln, and the other to the parson of Mölln, whensoever he died. And he asked to be buried in Christian man's burial, and to sing for his soul *placebo** and dirge, with masses and other good services after the custom and usages.

And then he showed to them a great chest that was well barred with iron, and four keys thereto belonging, and he told unto them that in that chest was all his good. And then he gave the chest to them to keep, that were right heavy for him. And then, within a month after his death, then the four should take the keys thereof, and open the chest, and deal all the money for his soul.

And within a while after, he departed. And when he was

* The Catholic prayer for the dead beginning *"placebo Domino in regione vivorum,"*

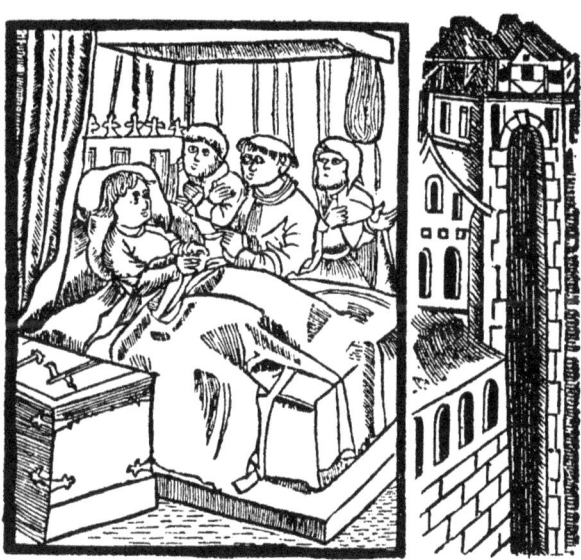

dead, they wound him in a winding sheet, and after in a coffin, and after on a bier. Then came the priests and fetched him to church and sang for him *placebo* and dirge. And in the mean time came in a sow with her pig and went over the bier, for she had found the taste of dead flesh, and with her nose she cast down the bier, whereof the priests and clerks were afraid. And they saw that it was down; then they ran so fast that each fell in another's neck for the thought that he had been risen again, and so they left him there. And then the sisters of a nunnery took the corpse and brought it to grave and buried it.

And when a month was past, then came the three parties for to unlock the chest and for to deal the money for his soul. And when that they had opened the chest, they found no other but stones therein. Then they wondered thereof, and the one looked on the other. And the parson had weened that the lords had had the money because they had the chest in keeping. And the lords weened that his friends had opened the chest and take out the treasure and put in stones the while that he was sick and so to have shut the chest again. And his friends weened that the curate had conveyed the treasure when that he confessed him.

And then in a great anger they departed from thence for, at the last, they knew that it was he that had done it for to mock them. And after that the lords and the curate agreed together again to bury him under the gallows, and so they did. And as they were delving of his grave, he stank so sore that they could not abide the air thereof. And so they covered him with earth again and let him lie still, and so they departed.

How Eulenspiegel was buried[*]

Thus, as Eulenspiegel was dead, then they brought him to be buried, and as they would have put the coffin into the pit

---

[*] There are two different stories about his burial, evidence that this is a collection of stories.

with two cords, the cord at the feet brake, so that the foot of the coffin fell into the bottom of the pit, and the coffin stood bolt upright in the midst of the grave. Then desired the people that stood about the grave that time, for the coffin to stand bolt upright. For in his lifetime, he was a very marvelous man, and he did many wonderful things, and shall be buried as marvelously. And in this manner, they left Eulenspiegel stand bolt upright in his grave, and they covered him with earth, and then they laid a stone.

And on the stone was graven and owl holding a glass with her claws.* And thereon was graven this scripture:

Presume no man away this stone to take,

For under this stone was Eulenspiegel buried late.

In the year of our Lord God, MCCC and fifty.

* Eulenspiegel literally means "owl mirror."

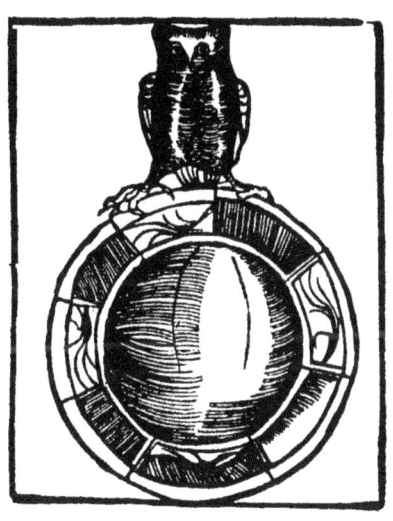

Printed in the USA
CPSIA information can be obtained
at www.ICGtesting.com
CBHW072233190924
14330CB00013B/43